THE KINGFISHER
SPACE
ENCYCLOPEDIA

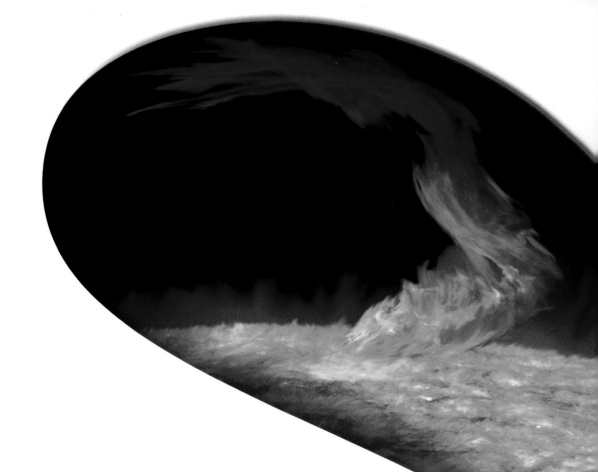

THE KINGFISHER
SPACE
ENCYCLOPEDIA

Dr. Mike Goldsmith

FELLOW OF THE BRITISH ROYAL ASTRONOMICAL SOCIETY

KINGFISHER
LONDON & NEW YORK

KINGFISHER
LONDON & NEW YORK

Distributed in the U.S. and Canada by Macmillan,
120 Broadway, New York, NY 10271

Library of Congress Cataloging-in-Publication data has been applied for.

ISBN: 978-0-7534-7664-2 (HB)
978-0-7534-7665-9 (PB)

Produced for Kingfisher by
Bender Richardson White, Uxbridge, England, U.K.
Editor: Lionel Bender
Design: Ben White
Cover design: Peter Clayman
Consultant: Stuart Atkinson

Kingfisher books are available for special promotions and premiums.
For details contact: Special Markets Department, Macmillan,
120 Broadway, New York, NY 10271.

For more information, please visit www.kingfisherbooks.com

Printed in China
1 3 5 7 9 8 6 4 2
1TR/1120/WKT/RV/128MA

Contents

INTRODUCTION

The universe—also known as the cosmos—is everything that there is, ever was, or will be. This book takes you on a journey through the universe, from the telescopes used on Earth to study the night sky to the farthest reaches of space and time.

The book is divided into five chapters: **Observing Space** explains how the universe appears from Earth and the ways that scientists (called astronomers) observe and examine it. **The Solar System** is about our solar system—which includes the Sun, Earth, seven other planets, and a whole range of other objects, from moons to dust grains. **Stars and Galaxies** takes you beyond the solar system to find out about stars and star groups, such as binaries, clusters, and galaxies. It also explains how stars form, change, and eventually die. **Space Exploration** describes how human beings have begun to explore the universe, both in crewed spacecraft and by the use of space telescopes and space robots. **Space in the Future** looks at the future of space exploration, at the amazing spacecraft and space colonies that may be built one day, and at the marvels and mysteries that lie ahead.

OBSERVING SPACE

Human beings have always been fascinated by the stars—
and puzzled by them, too. It has taken thousands of years
of study to understand them and our place among them.
Today, both amateur and highly trained professional
astronomers use a vast array of instruments and
equipment to continue this exploration.

Watching the sky

If you ever get the chance to look at the night sky on a moonless, cloudless night, far from any city lights, you might be amazed at what you see: a sky full of stars, together with occasional patches of misty light.

The human eye is amazing, but its use in astronomy is limited because of the vast distances involved. Over the past few hundred years, a whole range of devices have been invented to improve our view of the starry sky.

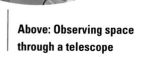

Above: Observing space through a telescope

The sky at night

The brightest object in the night sky is the Moon. Its brightness makes it hard to see many stars. When it is not in view, more than 1,000 stars can be seen with the naked eye. You might also see small misty patches that could be nebulae (see p.86), star clusters, or other galaxies. Over a few nights, five of the starlike objects called planets (see chapter 2) move around the sky.

Auroras

In the far northern and southern parts of the world, there are often bright colored lights seen in the night sky. They are called the northern lights, or aurora borealis—as shown below—in the north, and the southern lights, or aurora australis, in the south. They are caused by particles from the Sun crashing into Earth's magnetic field.

Sky gods and the night sky

Before the development of science, many people believed that the things they saw in the sky were controlled by gods. More than 2,000 years ago, the ancient Greeks saw patterns of stars that they associated with animals and the legends of their gods.

DAY AND NIGHT

We live on a spinning planet. As it turns, the Sun shines on different parts of it. It is daytime in the parts of the world on which the Sun shines, while elsewhere it is nighttime. The lengths of days and nights vary depending on where you live and the time of year.

PATHS OF THE SUN

Because Earth spins, we see the Sun move across the sky. On the equator, the Sun is seen above the horizon for 12 hours and disappears below it for another 12, and that pattern remains the same all year. In other parts of the world, the length of time that the Sun is seen in the sky changes with the seasons (see pp. 14–15).

A: The Sun's light is spread over a wide area, so it is colder here. People living here see the Sun low in the sky, even at noon.
B: Sunlight is spread over a smaller area, so it is warmer here. At noon, people living here see the Sun high up in the sky.

EARTH FACTS
- The Northern Hemisphere is the half of the world that is north of the equator.
- The Southern Hemisphere is the half of the world that is south of the equator.
- The equator is an imaginary line on Earth that is equal distance from the poles.
- The North Pole is one end of Earth's axis.
- The South Pole is the other end of Earth's axis.
- Earth's axis is the imaginary line around which Earth spins.
- The Arctic Circle is the southern limit of the 24-hour sunlit day.
- The Antarctic Circle is the northern limit of the 24-hour sunlit day.

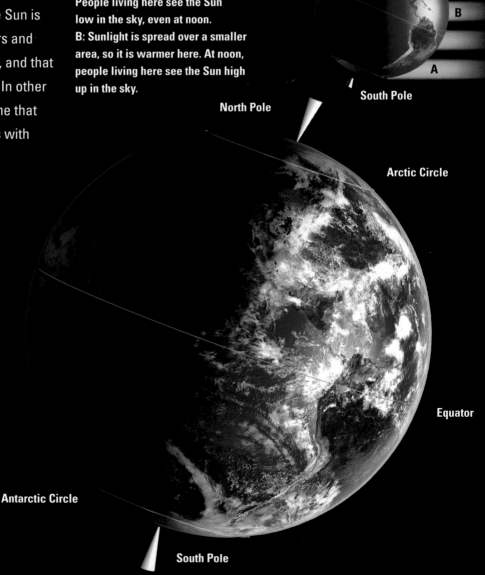

THE MIDNIGHT SUN

On the equator, the Sun passes directly overhead every day and the weather is hot all year. If you go far north or south of the equator, the Sun remains low in the sky all day, which is why it is colder there. Earth spins at an angle to the Sun so that at some times of the year Earth's North Pole leans toward the Sun. This means that northern parts of the world have long days and short nights. When it is midsummer in the Northern Hemisphere (which occurs in July), the days become so long in areas within the Arctic Circle that the Sun remains just above the horizon all night, even at midnight.

Below: A long-exposure photograph showing the movement of the Sun in the sky during an Arctic summer's night

The seasons

In many parts of the world, the weather changes throughout the year. In temperate regions, some months are hotter and others are colder. These different times of year are called seasons: summer is the hottest season and winter is the coldest.

In the Northern Hemisphere, winter begins on December 20 or 21, which has the longest night and shortest day of the year. Spring begins when the night is as long as the day (March 20 or 21), and summer begins on the longest day and shortest night (June 20 or 21).

What causes the seasons?

We have seasons because Earth's axis—the imaginary line that goes through the poles—is at an angle to the Sun. In July, the northern end of the axis leans toward the Sun, while the southern end leans away. This means that the Northern Hemisphere receives more sunlight at this time of year, so it is summer there. At the same time, it is winter in the Southern Hemisphere.

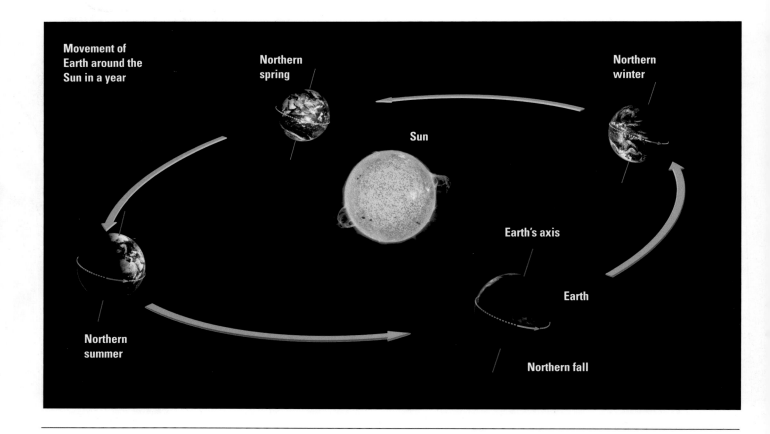

Movement of Earth around the Sun in a year

Northern spring

Sun

Northern winter

Earth's axis

Earth

Northern summer

Northern fall

Seasons and weather

Winter is cool partly because the days are short, so there is less time for the sunlight to warm things up. Also, the Sun is lower in the sky, which means that its light and heat are spread over a wider area.

Martian seasons

Earth is not the only planet with seasons. Mars also has an axis that is tilted at an angle to the Sun, which means that it has seasons, too. The effects of these seasons can be seen from Earth: when it is summer in the northern hemisphere of Mars, the polar icecap (seen here) shrinks, while the southern icecap grows.

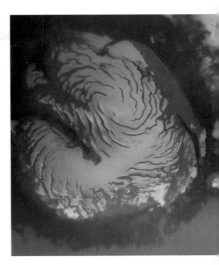

Animals in the winter

Winter can be a difficult time for animals because food is scarce. To cope with this, some birds and insects move to warmer areas (migrate) for the winter months. Some other animals hibernate, which means that they sleep for weeks or months at a time. Meanwhile, furry animals grow thicker coats to stay warm.

MYTHOLOGY

PROSERPINA
According to ancient Roman legends, Proserpina was kidnapped by Pluto, the god of the underworld. Proserpina's mother Ceres was the goddess of Earth. Ceres brought winter to the world, until Pluto sent Proserpina back to her. Ceres then allowed spring to return. But Proserpina still had to go back to the underworld once a year; that is why winter returns every year.

The turning sky

As Earth spins on its axis, the starry sky turns overhead. At different times of the night, some stars come into view, while others slip below the horizon. The stars visible to us change throughout the year, too.

The collections of stars that can be observed in the night sky also depend on where you live. There are many stars that can be seen only from certain parts of Earth.

The Southern Cross constellation

Polaris and the Southern Cross

If Earth's axis were extended out into space, it would pass close to a star called Polaris at one end and, at the other end, to a constellation called the Southern Cross. As Earth turns, Polaris hardly moves and the Southern Cross moves only slightly. Hence. they can be used to find north and south.

Navigating by the stars

Because the stars that are visible change depending on both time and place, they can be used to figure out the observer's position, by using clocks and star maps. This can be very useful at sea, where there are no landmarks to help.

Seasonal stars

Stars near Polaris can be seen all year long in the Northern Hemisphere, but other stars can be seen only at certain times of the year. This is because the night side of Earth faces different directions each season.

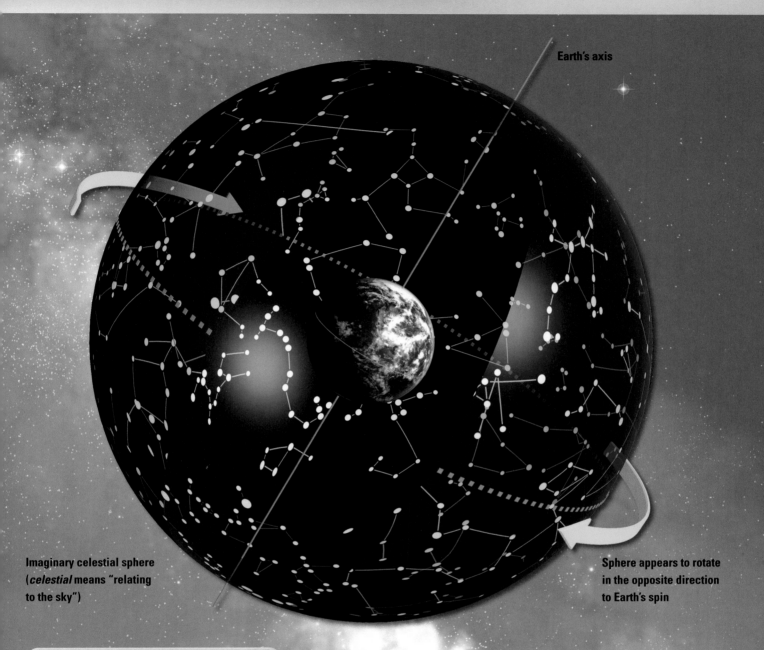

Earth's axis

Imaginary celestial sphere (*celestial* means "relating to the sky")

Sphere appears to rotate in the opposite direction to Earth's spin

The celestial sphere

Although the stars are actually at many different distances from Earth and do not move around it, it looks to us as if they are stuck on the inside of a rotating sphere, with Earth at its center. This imaginary sphere appears to turn from east to west, carrying the stars along with it.

ASTRONOMER

Tycho Brahe (1546–1601)
Tycho was a Danish astronomer whose observations of the stars and planets were the best that anyone had made up until the late 1500s. Tycho made thousands of measurements of the changing positions of the planets. His fellow astronomer Johannes Kepler used Tycho's observations to figure out the laws that describe the movements of the planets.

onstellations

thousands of years, people
ve connected the brightest stars
the sky to make patterns called
nstellations that resemble
ople, animals, and objects.

ay, constellations include all of the
s around the main patterns that we
every area of the night sky is part
one of 88 constellations.

Constellations near and far

It looks to us as if all of the stars in a
constellation are close together. But
in most cases, some of them are a
lot farther from us than others are.
They appear close only because they
are in roughly the same direction
from Earth.

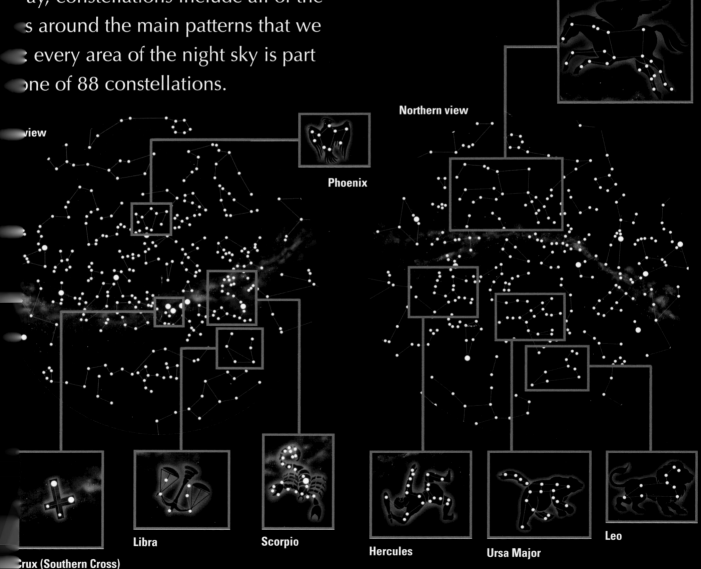

Pegasus

Northern view

Phoenix

view

Libra

Scorpio

Hercules

Ursa Major

Leo

rux (Southern Cross)

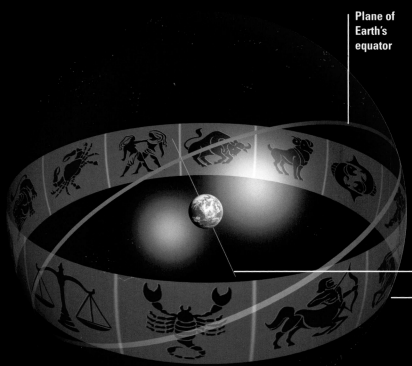

Plane of
Earth's
equator

The ecliptic

As you walk around a tree, its background changes. In the same way, as Earth moves around the Sun, its background of stars changes. To us, it looks like the Sun moves gradually around the celestial sphere every year. The path it takes is called the ecliptic. The ecliptic passes through all the zodiac constellations.

Earth's axis

Celestial sphere

The 12 signs of the zodiac are:

1. Capricorn	5. Taurus	9. Virgo
2. Aquarius	6. Gemini	10. Libra
3. Pisces	7. Cancer	11. Scorpio
4. Aries	8. Leo	12. Sagittarius

During the Renaissance—the rebirth of science from around 1400 to 1600—many artists created images of the night sky showing some of the signs of the zodiac.

The zodiac

Although we cannot see constellations during the day, they are still there in the sky, and the Sun passes in front of 12 of them during the year. These 12 constellations are called the signs of the zodiac and have been used for many centuries for fortunetelling. Many of the zodiac constellations are animals, and the Greek word *zodiac* means "circle of animals" in English.

MYTHOLOGY

ORION LEGENDS AND MYTHS

There are legends about the constellation of Orion in many cultures. In ancient Greece, he was a mythical hunter whom the god Zeus placed in the heavens, while the Khoisan people of Africa think of the three stars in Orion's belt as being three zebras. In Japan, the stars are said to form the shape of a traditional drum called a *tsuzumi*.

Eclipses

In an eclipse, a heavenly body such as a planet or moon blocks light from a star. In a solar eclipse, the Moon blocks sunlight. In a lunar eclipse, Earth blocks sunlight.

Many ancient civilizations regarded eclipses as signs that terrible events would occur. Today, we know that the explanation for them is simple: solar eclipses happen when the Moon's shadow falls on Earth, and lunar eclipses happen when Earth's shadow falls on the Moon.

USEFUL ECLIPSES
Eclipses are useful as well as exciting. During a solar eclipse, the Sun's outer atmosphere, called the corona, can be seen and studied—usually it is lost in the glare of the Sun. And, when people in history mention eclipses, their writings can be dated exactly because astronomers know when every historical eclipse took place.

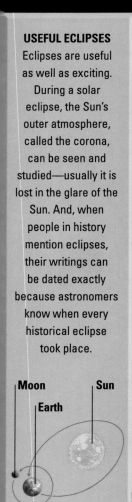

Moon Sun
Earth

World of eclipses

Earth is the only planet from which a total solar eclipse can be seen. This is because our moon happens to be about 400 times smaller than the Sun and also about 400 times closer to us. So the sizes of the Sun and Moon in the sky are almost the same. Because of this, the Moon can completely cover the Sun during an eclipse.

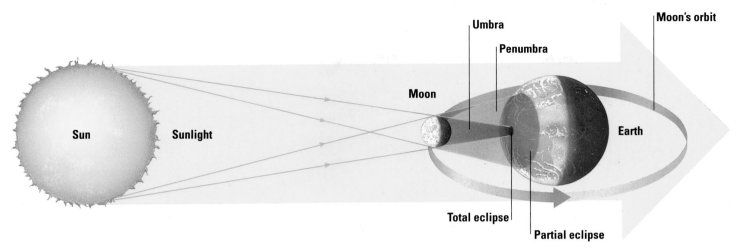

Solar eclipses

Solar eclipses can be seen only from those parts of Earth where the Moon's shadow falls. People in the umbra (complete shadow) see a total eclipse because the Sun is completely covered by the Moon, while those in the penumbra (shadow's edsge) see only part of the Sun blacked out: a partial eclipse.

Eclipses on other planets

Although total solar eclipses happen only on Earth, partial ones can be seen from many planets. This is a partial eclipse of the Sun by the Martian moon Phobos, as seen by the Mars rover *Opportunity*.

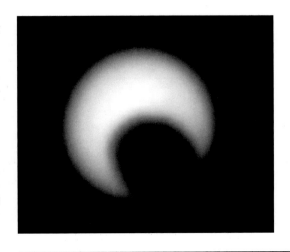

Lunar eclipses

Lunar eclipses happen more often than solar ones and can be seen from anywhere on Earth that the Moon is visible. During a total lunar eclipse, the Moon turns red. This is because, although Earth's shadow cuts off direct sunlight from the Moon, some red light from the Sun is bent toward the Moon by our atmosphere. During a partial lunar eclipse, the shaded part of the moon looks dark gray or black.

Power of the eclipse

It is said that Christopher Columbus's knowledge of an upcoming lunar eclipse in 1504 was a lifesaver. When he argued with Jamaican islanders who had refused his crew food and water, Columbus claimed that he had power over the Moon and threatened to remove it from the sky. When the islanders still refused, the Moon began to vanish, returning only when Columbus ordered it to—by which time the worried islanders had provided the supplies.

RADIATION FROM SPACE

LIGHT IS ONLY ONE OF MANY TYPES OF RADIATION THAT THE SUN, STARS, AND OTHER OBJECTS SEND OUT INTO SPACE. ALTHOUGH WE CANNOT SEE THE OTHER KINDS, THERE ARE INSTRUMENTS THAT CAN DETECT THEM AND MAKE MAPS AND PICTURES FOR US.

USING RADIATION

We use different types of radiation for different things. This diagram shows some of them:

• Long-wavelength radio waves are used for radio broadcasts.

• Shorter radio waves are used for TV broadcasts.

• Very short radio waves are used in radar systems.

• The shortest radio waves, also called microwaves, are used to cook food.

• Infrared waves are used in sensors and remote controls.

• Visible light allows us to see.

• Tanning beds use ultraviolet radiation.

• X-rays allow us to look inside the human body.

• Gamma rays are so powerful that they can look inside metal objects such as jet engines.

THE ELECTROMAGNETIC SPECTRUM

The electromagnetic spectrum includes all of the different types of radiation, including visible light. All radiation travels as if it is made of waves. The different types of radiation differ according to the lengths of their waves. Radio waves have the longest waves, then infrared, followed by visible light, ultraviolet, x-rays, and gamma rays. The shorter the wavelength of radiation, the more powerful it can be.

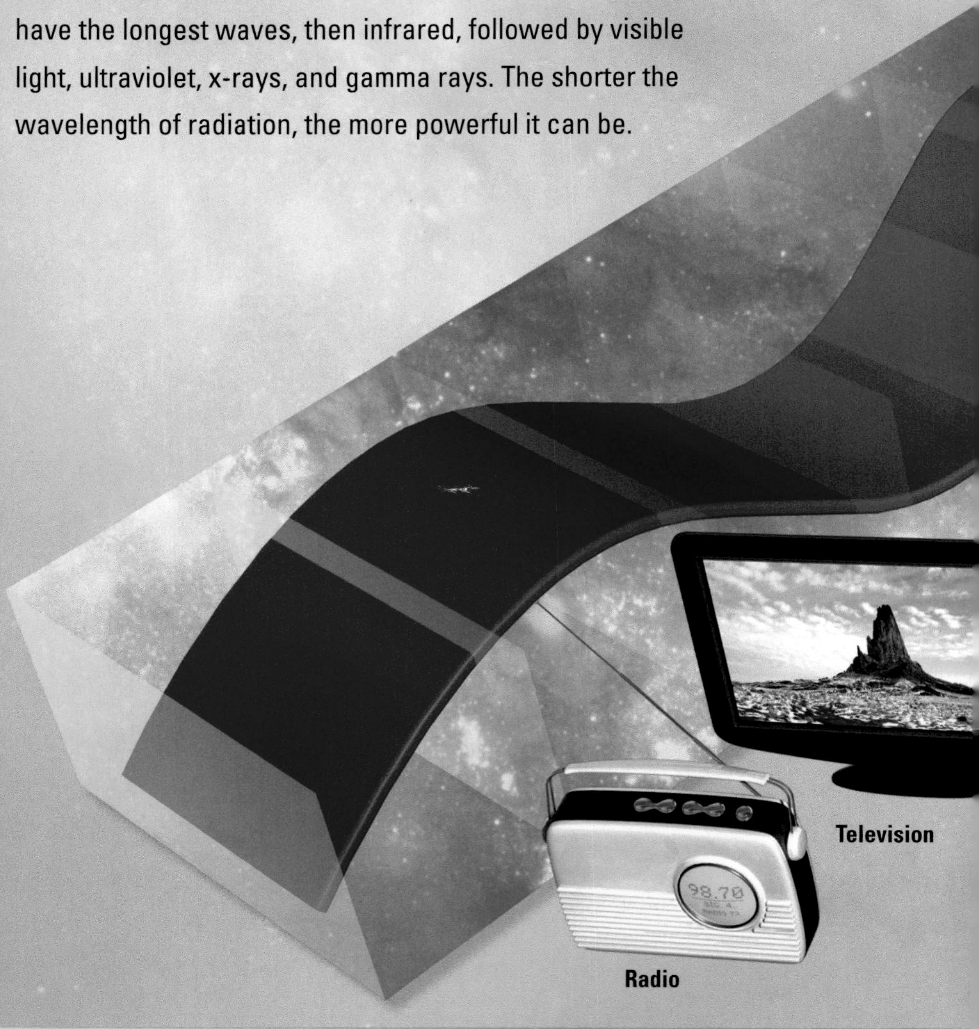

Television

98.70

Radio

THE VISIBLE SPECTRUM

White light is made up of various colors of light. We can see this when raindrops split white sunlight into colors to make a rainbow. The colors in a rainbow are arranged in order of their wavelengths, from long-wavelength red light to short-wavelength violet light.

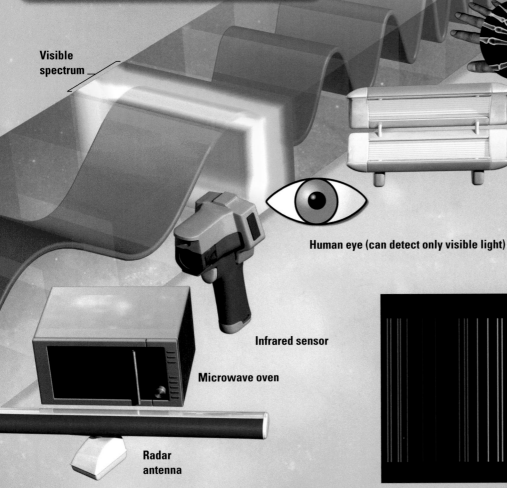

Visible spectrum

Gamma-ray image of a jet engine

X-ray image of a hand

Ultraviolet tanning bed

Human eye (can detect only visible light)

Infrared sensor

Microwave oven

Radar antenna

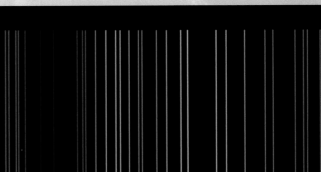

HEAT RAYS

A prism is a piece of glass that breaks up light into its spectrum of colors. Astronomer William Herschel (1738–1822) used a prism to make a spectrum of sunlight and then placed a thermometer just beyond the red end. The thermometer indicated that heat was present: Herschel had discovered invisible infrared radiation.

LINE SPECTRA

Sometimes, when light from an object in space is spread out, it does not make a broad band of color like a rainbow. Instead, groups of colored lines appear. These are called spectral lines, and they can tell astronomers what the object is made of, how hot it is, how fast it is moving, and even how strong its magnetic field is.

Optical telescopes

The majority of the objects that astronomers look at are very dim—too dim to be seen with the naked eye. Optical telescopes make these objects appear closer and brighter.

To capture as much light as possible, the best telescopes use huge mirrors or pieces of shaped glass called lenses. These are made very carefully so that they are extremely smooth and have exactly the right shape.

What is a telescope?

A telescope is an instrument used for studying distant objects. A good optical telescope needs a well-made primary (main) lens or mirror, and some have a special camera or other device to make an image or measurements of the objects it studies. Electric motors are used to move and point a telescope in the right direction and then to keep it moving slowly at exactly the right speed so that it keeps up with the stars as the sky turns.

EARLY TELESCOPES

1609
First astronomical telescope, built by Galileo Galilei

1688
First reflector, built by Sir Isaac Newton

1845
Leviathan becomes the largest telescope built for more than 50 years, 6 ft. (1.83m) across. Built by William Parsons (Lord Rosse)

Herschel's telescope

Astronomer William Herschel built more than 400 telescopes. The one below had a mirror 4.1 ft. (1.26m) across, and the first time he used it, Herschel discovered a new moon of Saturn.

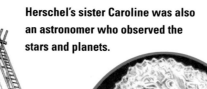

Herschel's sister Caroline was also an astronomer who observed the stars and planets.

Refractors

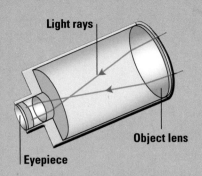

Light rays

Object lens

Eyepiece

Refractors are telescopes that use lenses to gather light. They are tougher than reflectors (see below) and are often used by amateur astronomers, but the lenses are very heavy: if they are more than around 3 ft. (1m) across, they sag under their own weight.

Giant telescope

The Very Large Telescope (VLT) observatory in the Atacama Desert, Chile, is a facility home to four reflector telescopes called Unit Telescopes (UTs). Each UT has a main mirror 27 ft. (8.2m) across, and four secondary mirrors 5.9 ft (1.8m) across.

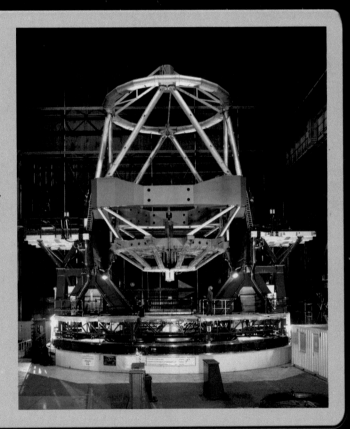

Left: A laser is used to make a target high up in the sky for telescopes to focus on.

Reflectors

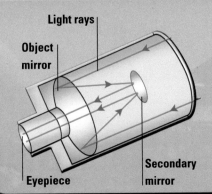

Light rays

Object mirror

Eyepiece

Secondary mirror

All of the world's largest telescopes are reflectors that use a curved mirror to capture light. A secondary mirror sends the light to a smaller lens called an eyepiece. The eyepiece focuses the light onto the eye or recording instrument.

Radio telescopes

The universe is full of radio waves, but people discovered them only in 1887, and radio astronomy did not begin until 1932.

Because radio waves are so long, the instruments that detect them have to be large. Even a small radio-telescope dish is larger than the primary lens or mirror of an optical telescope.

How radio telescopes work

The dish of a radio telescope is designed so that radio waves are reflected by it to a single point above the disk's center, called the focus. A subreflector at this point picks up the radio waves and sends them to a detector. Then they are amplified, or made stronger.

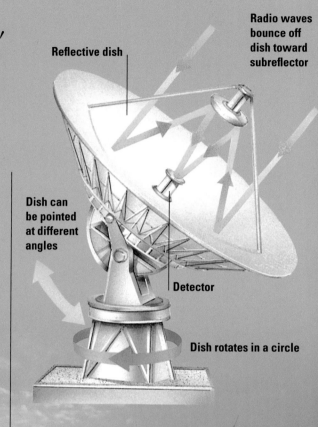

Radio waves bounce off dish toward subreflector

Reflective dish

Dish can be pointed at different angles

Detector

Dish rotates in a circle

Arrays

Rather than making one huge radio telescope, it is often easier to make several of them point at the same object and join all of the results together. This is called an array.

Linking telescopes

Earth-rotation synthesis is a way of making arrays of radio telescopes work together even better. If they all point at the same object in the sky for many hours, the rotation of Earth means that they each provide a range of views from different points. Using computers, the views are combined to produce an improved image.

Radio windows

Most radio waves (shown above as blue) travel through the atmosphere as easily as light rays (multicolored). The only radio waves that do not pass through are either very short or longer than 330 ft. (100m) (purple). A layer in the atmosphere called the ionosphere stops these waves. The ionosphere is useful to us because it can be used to bounce our own radio messages from one part of Earth to another.

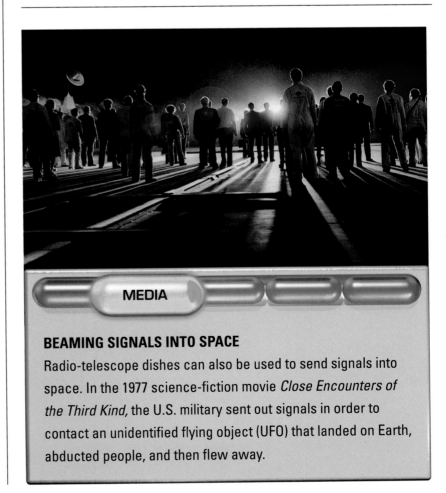

Accidental astronomer

Karl Jansky (1905–1950) became the first radio astronomer when he detected radio waves from the Milky Way (see pp. 88–89) in 1931. He was looking for sources of noise called static that interfere with radio broadcasts, using a radio detector that he had constructed. It could be turned, which helped pinpoint the sources of radio signals.

MEDIA

BEAMING SIGNALS INTO SPACE

Radio-telescope dishes can also be used to send signals into space. In the 1977 science-fiction movie *Close Encounters of the Third Kind,* the U.S. military sent out signals in order to contact an unidentified flying object (UFO) that landed on Earth, abducted people, and then flew away.

Terrestrial observatories

Observatories are special sites from which to view the night sky. People set up the first observatories thousands of years ago. Once the telescope was invented in the 1600s, new observatories were set up, first in Europe, then in the U.S.

From the late 1600s onward, many nations competed to build bigger and better observatories. The observations made at those sites were used both to study the universe and to measure time accurately.

What is an observatory like?

Most terrestrial, or ground-based, observatories contain optical and infrared telescopes. So that the stars can be seen clearly, these observatories are located in parts of the world where the air is as clear and cloudless as possible, far from city lights. They are usually built on high mountains, because the air is thinner and cleaner there. The telescopes and other delicate equipment are protected from the weather by movable domes, with slits in them through which the telescopes can observe the sky.

OBSERVATORY SITES
Mount Graham International Observatory, Arizona: includes the Large Binocular Telescope, one of the world's most powerful optical telescopes

Laser Interferometer Gravitational-Wave Observatory, Louisiana: the most sensitive experimental gravitational-wave observatory

Super-Kamiokande, Mount Kamioka, Japan: one of the most successful neutrino observatories

Below: Several observatories share the heights of Mauna Kea in Hawaii, including the Keck.

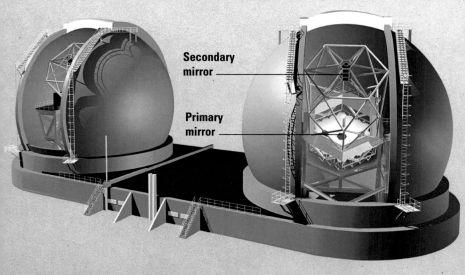

Secondary mirror

Primary mirror

Keck Observatory

The W. M. Keck Observatory was built on an extinct volcano in Hawaii. Its twin telescopes have mirrors 33 ft. (10m) across. Each mirror is made of 36 smaller mirrors, all of which can move separately. Using a technique called interferometry, the two telescopes can work together to make better observations than each could alone.

Detecting gravitational waves

When objects move, they make tiny wobbles in the time and space around them, which spread out like ripples. These ripples are called gravitational waves. In 2016, the internationally funded Advanced Laser Interferometer Gravitational-Wave Observatory (LIGO) announced the first observations of gravitational waves, made by colliding black holes over one billion light-years away.

Neutrino telescopes

Neutrinos are tiny particles that hurtle through space in huge numbers. Because they pass through almost anything, they are almost impossible to detect. Several neutrino telescopes have been built down old mines, where no other form of radiation can penetrate. Each includes vast amounts of liquid. Occasionally, a neutrino changes the liquid slightly, and this change triggers sensitive detectors.

SPACE OBSERVATORIES

PUTTING AN OBSERVATORY IN ORBIT IS A MAJOR FEAT, BUT IT IS THE ONLY WAY TO MAKE OBSERVATIONS OF SOME TYPES OF RADIATION. THIS IS BECAUSE EARTH'S ATMOSPHERE BLOCKS THEM OUT BEFORE THEY CAN REACH THE GROUND.

Satellite

Space shuttle

Aurora

Meteors

Weather balloon

Passenger plane

A view through the atmosphere

WHERE SPACE STARTS

Space is often defined as starting at 60 mi. (100km) above Earth, but there is no sudden beginning to space: as you rise higher and higher from Earth, the air gets gradually thinner. The thinner the air, the more radiation is available to observe, so balloons, planes, and the space shuttle have all been used as temporary observatories. However, it is necessary to reach a height of about 190 mi. (300km) in order to put a space observatory satellite in orbit. Only there is the air thin enough not to slow down the observatory and cause it to crash back to Earth.

The space shuttle *Endeavour* approaches the Hubble Space Telescope to repair it.

ATMOSPHERIC EFFECTS

The atmosphere causes many problems for ground-based telescopes. First of all, it is often full of clouds that make most observations impossible. Even when there are no clouds, the air is in constant motion, which limits the types of observations that can be made. This motion is why stars twinkle: in space, they shine steadily. And there are many types of radiation that the air itself blocks, including most infrared and ultraviolet and practically all x-rays and gamma rays.

HUBBLE VISION

The Hubble Space Telescope has provided us with some of the best views of planets, galaxies, and other objects in space. But it was almost a complete failure—a tiny error in the construction of its main mirror led to blurry images. So, in 1993, a space shuttle was sent to repair it. It was one of the most challenging shuttle missions, but it was a success.

Great astronomers

There are two kinds of astronomers—observational astronomers watch and measure the stars, and theoretical astronomers develop mathematical theories to explain how the universe and its contents work.

Galileo Galilei (1564–1642)

Galileo was an Italian scientist who, in 1609, was the first person to use a telescope to study the night sky. Within a few hours, he had found out what the surface of our Moon looks like. He also discovered four moons in orbit around the planet Jupiter. In 1610, he was the first to see that the Milky Way is made of stars. Galileo was also an important theoretical astronomer, explaining sunspots and comets and trying to prove that Earth orbits the Sun. Though not all of his conclusions were correct, it was he who really began the modern science of astronomy.

Sir Isaac Newton (1643–1727)

Newton invented the reflecting telescope, which became the most useful astronomical instrument for centuries. His theories correctly explained the motions of the Moon, planets, and comets for the first time. Newton proved that the Moon orbits Earth because of the force of gravity. He figured out the mathematics that describes how gravity changes depending on the masses and distances of the objects involved. He also showed how to use his laws of gravity and of motion to determine the movements of planets and comets.

Edwin Hubble (1889–1953)

Hubble, along with his colleagues, made two of the greatest scientific discoveries of the 1900s. The first was that the enormous group of stars (called the Milky Way galaxy), of which the Sun is a member, is one of many similar systems. This showed that the universe is much larger than had previously been believed. The second discovery was that the entire universe is expanding. This suggested that the universe had come into existence long ago and had been expanding from then on, rather than having always existed.

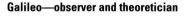

Galileo—observer and theoretician

Newton—theoretician

Hubble—observer and theoretician

WEBSITES ABOUT SPACE AND TIME

http://apod.nasa.gov/apod/astropix.html   A new astronomy picture every day.

http://eclipse.gsfc.nasa.gov/eclipse.html   Past and future eclipses.

http://skyview.gsfc.nasa.gov   A virtual observatory.

www.popastro.com/youngstargazers/skyguide/index.php   Looks at what is visible in the sky every night.

www.windows2Universe.org/mythology/stars.html   Myths and legends of the stars.

THE SOLAR SYSTEM

Earth, the Sun, and the Moon are all members of the
solar system, along with seven other planets, many moons,
comets, asteroids, and meteoroids. The planets occupy
only a small area in the middle of the solar system. Around
them is the Kuiper belt and then a vast cloud containing
billions of pieces of rock and ice.

The Sun and its planets

The Sun is at the center of the solar system. It is more massive than all of the planets put together. Everything in the solar system is moving, and everything moves around the Sun or some other astronomical object.

There are three types of planets in the solar system. The inner four are the rocky, or terrestrial (Earthlike), planets: Mercury, Venus, Earth, and Mars. They are made of rock and metal. Jupiter and Saturn are gas giants, with rings, deep cloudy atmospheres, and many moons. The last two planets, Uranus and Neptune, are ice giants.

Discovering the solar system

Five planets, along with the Sun and the Moon, can easily be seen in the sky without a telescope. Bright comets were also known, although it was later realized that these were beyond our atmosphere. So, until the first telescopes were made in the 1600s, the rest of the solar system was invisible and unknown. Since then, two more planets and many moons and comets have been discovered. A number of them have been visited by spacecraft from Earth.

Gravity

Gravity is the force that holds you to the ground and keeps the planets moving around the Sun. Each object pulls on every other object with the force of gravity. But only large objects such as moons and planets are massive enough for their gravity to be noticeable.

PLANET KEY

1. Mercury
2. Venus
3. Earth
4. Mars
5. Jupiter
6. Saturn
7. Uranus
8. Neptune

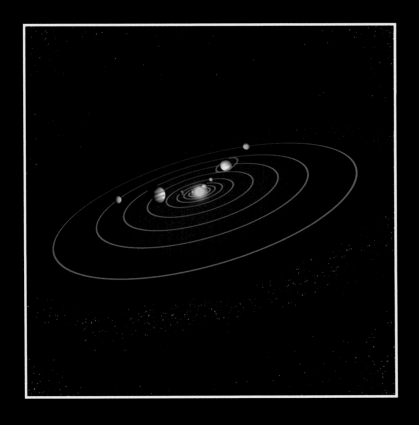

Orbits and years

The Sun's gravity pulls harder on planets close to it, so those planets must orbit (go around) it quickly in order to avoid being pulled in. The time taken for a planet to orbit the Sun once is its year. So, because inner planets travel fast—and also because their orbits are small—their years are short.

6

7

8

HOW THE SYSTEM FORMED

THE SOLAR SYSTEM BEGAN TO FORM ABOUT 4.6 BILLION YEARS AGO, INSIDE A HUGE, DARK SPACE CLOUD. THE CLOUD WAS DISTURBED BY A SUPERNOVA (SEE P. 75), AND PARTS OF IT COLLAPSED. ONE OF THESE AREAS EVENTUALLY FORMED THE SUN AND PLANETS.

CLOUD COLLAPSE

Once a part of the cloud started to collapse, the gravity pull of its particles drew it tightly together. As it shrank, it began to spin and formed a disk in space. In the middle of the disk, the cloud material became closely packed and hot, forming a proto-Sun.

THE YOUNG SUN

The particles in the core of the disk were so tightly packed together that they kept crashing into one another, and this made them get hotter and hotter. Eventually, they were so hot that the core of the disk started to glow with light and heat. The core was now a baby version of the Sun, called a T Tauri star.

NEW WORLDS

The T Tauri star kept getting hotter until nuclear reactions began in its core (see pp. 68–69). It was now a true star. Meanwhile, material in the rest of the spinning disk gathered together because of the pull of gravity. The material formed rings that later turned into many planets—perhaps as many as 30.

DESTRUCTION

Many of the newborn planets crashed into one another. Sometimes, they stuck together to form new, larger planets. In other cases, they destroyed one another. Eventually, only the eight planets we know today remained. Some of them captured wandering small worlds that went into orbit around them as moons.

Mercury

Mercury is the smallest planet and the closest to the Sun. Because Mercury has a thin atmosphere, heat escapes from it quickly. After the Sun sets on Mercury, its nights are cold.

The Sun is so close to Mercury that it shines very brightly there: more than six times as brightly as on Earth. The very thin atmosphere means that the sky is black.

Left: Mercury is covered in craters caused by impacts from space objects.

MERCURY FACTS
Discoverer
Unknown
Discovery date
Prehistoric
Average distance from the Sun
36 million mi.
(58 million km)
Year length
87.97 Earth days
Rotation period
58.65 Earth days
Equatorial radius
1,516 mi. (2,440km)
(38% of Earth)
First reached
1974, by *Mariner 10*
Gravity compared with Earth
38%
Main atmospheric gases
Oxygen (42%)
Sodium (29%)
Hydrogen (22%)
Helium (6%)
Potassium (1%)
Number of moons
0

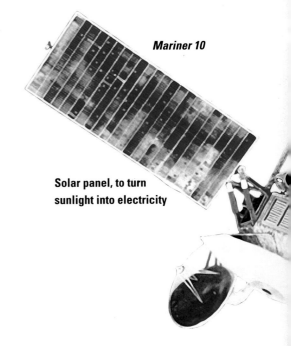

Mariner 10

Solar panel, to turn sunlight into electricity

Mercury overview

Mercury spins very slowly, which means that it has very long days and nights. It also has a very short year—it does not even last for two Mercurian days. It is so hot on Mercury that some metals, such as tin and lead, would melt there. Like Earth, Mercury has an internal magnetic field that acts like an enormous bar magnet with a north and south pole. The *MESSENGER* probe discovered that the center of Mercury's field is far to the north of the planet's center.

Missions to Mercury

Only two spacecraft have traveled to Mercury. *Mariner 10* flew past the planet three times in 1974 and 1975. It took photos of about half of the surface. The second probe, *MESSENGER*, was launched in August 2004 and was deliberately crashed into Mercury in April 2015. Its name reflects the studies it made—*ME*rcury *S*urface, *S*pace *EN*vironment, *GE*ochemistry, and *R*anging. It made detailed maps of the planet, and discovered ice there.

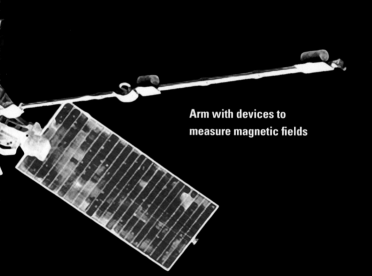

Arm with devices to measure magnetic fields

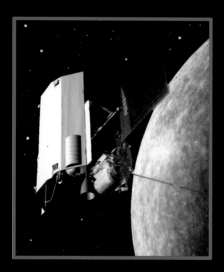

Right: *MESSENGER* probe above the surface of Mercury

Weird world

Mariner 10 discovered a huge crater on Mercury that was then named Caloris Basin. It was formed billions of years ago when an enormous object struck Mercury. The impact was so powerful that shock waves traveled through the whole planet. At the opposite side of Mercury to the basin is a strange, jumbled landscape, where the shock waves met up again.

MYTHOLOGY

PLANET GOD

All of the planets are named after Roman and Greek gods. Mercury was supposed to be a fast-moving Roman god with wings on his shoes and on his hat, too—a great name for the fastest planet. He was also the messenger of the other gods and delivered dreams to people as they slept.

Venus

Venus is the planet that comes closest to Earth, and because it is also close to the Sun and covered in bright clouds, it often shines brightly in our sky.

The surface of Venus is dark and very hot. Drops of acid fall from the clouds, and lightning often flashes in the orange-yellow sky.

Venus overview

On Venus, the days last longer than the years. On the surface, the Sun is never seen. The temperature is almost the same all day and night—all year and all over the planet.

VENUS FACTS
Discoverer
Unknown
Discovery date
Prehistoric
Average distance from the Sun
67 million mi.
(108 million km)
Year length
224.70 Earth days
Rotation period
243.02 Earth days
Equatorial radius
3,761 mi. (6,052km)
(95% of Earth)
First reached
1962, by *Mariner 2*
Gravity compared with Earth
90%
Main atmospheric gases
Carbon dioxide (96%)
Nitrogen (4%)
Number of moons
0

Maat Mons is shown in this computer-generated three-dimensional perspective of the surface of Venus.

Below: *Magellan* made radar maps of Venus.

Radar antennae

Missions to Venus

Many spacecraft have visited Venus, but landers are quickly destroyed by the dangerous atmosphere there. However, some have sent photos and information back to Earth first.

Volcanoes on Venus

Venus has hundreds of volcanoes, some of which are possibly still active. Some volcanoes are called arachnoids because they are surrounded by patterns of ridges that make them look like spiders.

About 80% of sunlight is reflected.

Each of the three cloud layers contains a different size of sulfuric acid droplets.

Infrared is caught by carbon dioxide in the atmosphere, making it hotter.

The surface is heated by sunlight, making it glow with infrared radiation.

Only 20% of sunlight reaches the surface.

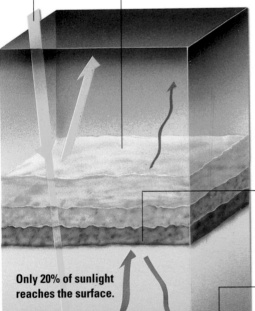

Atmosphere

Although it is not the closest planet to the Sun, Venus is the hottest one. This is because of its atmosphere, which contains gases that trap the Sun's heat. This is known as the greenhouse effect.

HISTORY

TRANSITS OF VENUS

When Venus passes directly between Earth and the Sun, it can be seen as a black dot on the Sun's face. This is called a transit. Expeditions were once sent to distant parts of the world to observe transits, as this allowed the distance from Earth to the Sun to be figured out.

Earth

Earth, our home in space, is the third planet from the Sun and the only one with oceans on its surface. As far as we know, it is the only planet on which life exists.

EARTH FACTS

Average distance from the Sun
93 million mi.
(150 million km)

Year length
365 or 366 days:
average 365.26 days

Rotation period
23.93 hours

Equatorial radius
3,963 mi. (6,378km)

Mass
13.16 trillion trillion lb.
(5.97 trillion trillion kg)

Average density
344 lb. per cubic foot
(5,515kg per cubic meter)

Gravitational acceleration near surface
32 ft. (9.81m) per second per second

Main atmospheric gases
Nitrogen (78%)
Oxygen (21%)
Trace gases (1%)

Number of moons
1

For thousands of years, people thought that Earth was the center of the universe. It was only in the 1500s that scientists proved that it is actually a planet in constant orbit around the Sun.

Below: From the International Space Station, Earth can be seen as a shining blue and white planet.

Earth overview

Earth is the densest planet in the solar system—that is, it has the most mass squeezed into its volume. It also has the largest moon in proportion to its own size and a strong magnetic field. This magnetic field is essential to us, as it protects Earth from the disruptive effects of solar wind (see p. 71). We are also protected by Earth's atmosphere, which stops most dangerous types of radiation from reaching the surface.

Inside Earth

The outer layer of Earth, on which we live, is called the crust. It covers the entire planet and extends under the oceans. Underneath it is a thick rocky layer called the mantle, and beneath that is the core. The core is extremely hot and made mostly of the metals iron and nickel.

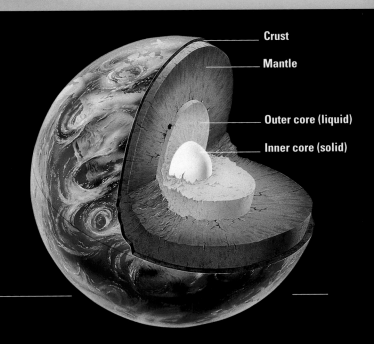

Crust

Mantle

Outer core (liquid)

Inner core (solid)

Why is there life on Earth?

Living things were able to evolve on Earth for two main reasons: our planet has enough mass to hold on to a thick atmosphere, and it is the right temperature for water to be a liquid in some places.

The Moon

The Moon is by far the closest astronomical object to us. It shines by reflecting sunlight onto Earth. The part of the Moon lit by the Sun changes as the Moon moves, which is why it seems to change its shape.

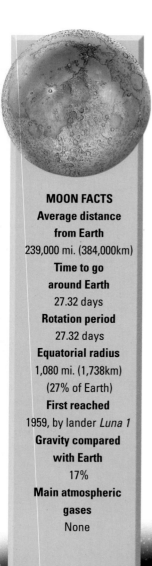

MOON FACTS
Average distance from Earth
239,000 mi. (384,000km)
Time to go around Earth
27.32 days
Rotation period
27.32 days
Equatorial radius
1,080 mi. (1,738km)
(27% of Earth)
First reached
1959, by lander *Luna 1*
Gravity compared with Earth
17%
Main atmospheric gases
None

Because the Moon is so small and light, its gravity pull is very weak. This means that astronauts on the Moon weigh about one-sixth of the amount that they do on Earth.

World without weather

The weak lunar gravity means that the Moon cannot hold on to an atmosphere. This lack of atmosphere means that there is no weather on the Moon. Because of this, the footprints left by astronauts in the 1960s are still there.

Moon birth

The Moon is 4.5 billion years old—almost as old as Earth. It was formed as the result of a small planet named Theia crashing into Earth. The planet was destroyed. Rubble from it and Earth was thrown into orbit, and the Moon formed from this rubble. Since then, the Moon has slowly moved away from Earth. It is now retreating at the same speed as your fingernails grow.

Left: *Surveyor 3* **landed on the Moon in 1967.**

The hidden face

As the Moon moves around Earth, it turns at exactly the same rate. This means that it always shows us the same side. The far side can be seen only by spacecraft. It looks very different from the near side, as it has no large "seas."

Moonscape

From Earth, we can see huge dark patches on the Moon. These are called seas but are actually plains of cold, hard lava. Brighter patches are mountainous areas. The Moon is covered in bowl-shaped depressions called craters. These were caused by huge objects crashing into its surface.

Tides

As the Moon moves around Earth, it pulls on our oceans with the force of gravity. Together with the Sun's gravity, this causes tides. When the Sun and Moon pull in the same direction, tides are at their highest.

Mars

In some ways, Mars is a lot like Earth. Its day is almost the same length, its temperature is not much lower, and some of its weather is similar, too.

MARS FACTS
Discoverer
Unknown
Discovery date
Prehistoric
Average distance from the Sun
142 million mi.
(228 million km)
Year length
1.88 Earth years
Rotation period
24.6 hours
Equatorial radius
2,110 mi. (3,396km)
(53% of Earth)
First reached
1965, by *Mariner 4*
Gravity compared with Earth
38%
Main atmospheric gases
Carbon dioxide (95%)
Nitrogen (3%)
Argon (2%)
Number of moons
2

The temperature on the surface of Mars changes throughout the year, partly because it has seasons (see p. 15) but also because it has an oval orbit, which means that its distance from the Sun varies greatly.

Mars as it was about 4 billion years ago.

Deimos

Phobos

Phobos and *Deimos* are Greek words meaning "fear" and "terror."

Mars overview

Mars is the fourth and final rocky planet from the Sun. It is covered in deserts, with huge canyons much larger than those on Earth. The soil is reddish because the iron in it has turned to rust. Its atmosphere is very thin. When the planet is coldest, about one-third of the atmosphere freezes solid.

Mars moons

Mars has two tiny moons—Phobos and Deimos—that are two of the darkest objects in the solar system. They are probably asteroids (see p. 58) that have been trapped by the gravity of Mars. Both moons always keep the same face turned toward Mars.

Exploring Mars

Mars is the best known of the planets because its surface can be seen by Earth-based telescopes, and it has been explored by more spacecraft than any other planet. The above picture was taken by the *Pathfinder* lander and shows the *Sojourner* rover beside a big boulder.

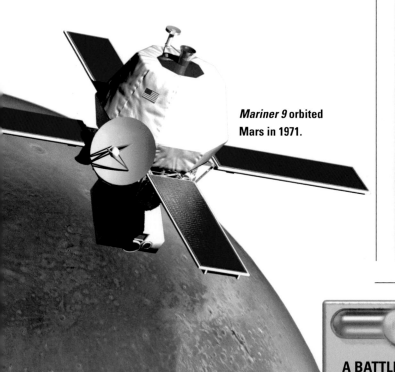

Mariner 9 orbited Mars in 1971.

Volcanoes on Mars

There are several volcanoes on Mars, including the largest in the solar system, Olympus Mons. It is three times the height of Mount Everest and covers an area the size of Ireland. It is thought to have last erupted about 25 million years ago.

MEDIA

A BATTLE BETWEEN EARTH AND MARS

In 1898, H. G. Wells wrote *The War of the Worlds*, a story about an invasion of Earth from Mars. In it, Martians conquer Earth but are then destroyed by germs in our atmosphere. When a radio version of this story was broadcast in the U.S. in 1938, some people thought it was a real report and panicked.

LIFE ON MARS

Ever since astronomers thought they saw canals on Mars in the late 1800s, people have searched for life there. First they used telescopes and then spacecraft, landers, and rovers.

Water must have flowed over the surface of Mars for a long time.

WATER ON MARS

The canals of Mars were not real, but there are riverbeds there through which water once flowed, long ago when the atmosphere of Mars was thicker than it is now. The presence of water makes it more likely that life once existed on Mars. This area of the planet (right) was carved out by water about a million years ago. The picture was taken by the Mars *Reconnaissance* orbiter.

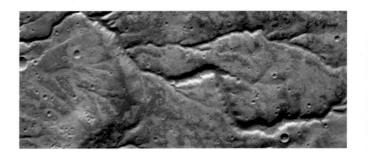

MARTIAN ICE

In 2008, a crater was found near the north pole of Mars with ice covering part of its floor. This ice never melts. Maybe future astronauts will use it for drinking water.

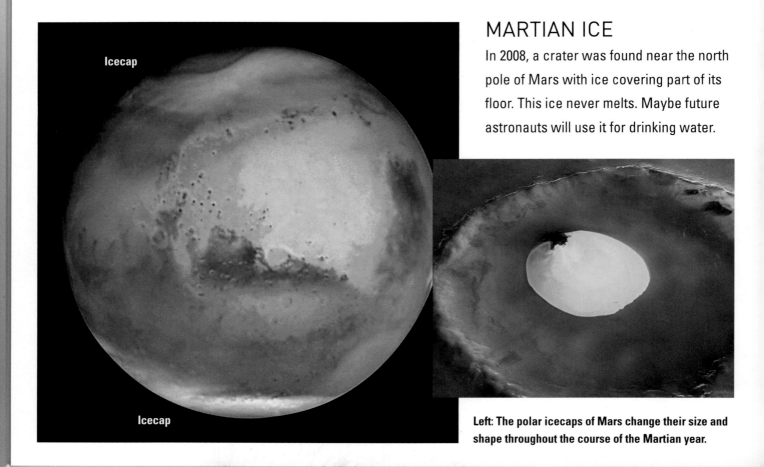

Icecap

Icecap

Left: The polar icecaps of Mars change their size and shape throughout the course of the Martian year.

LANDERS AND ROVERS

Six landers and four rovers have landed successfully on Mars. The first was *Mars 3* in 1971, which only worked for a few seconds before failing. Next were the *Viking* landers (one shown right), which discovered strange chemical activity in the soil in 1977. The *Sojourner* rover studied the Martian soil and atmosphere in 1997. *Spirit* and *Opportunity* arrived in 2004 and proved that liquid water once flowed on Mars; the *Phoenix* lander found ice there in 2008. The rover, *Curiosity*, landed on Mars in 2012, and the latest lander, *InSight*, landed in 2018.

Curiosity has a robotic arm, six wheels, and 17 cameras.

Jupiter

By far the largest and most massive planet, Jupiter is the fifth from the Sun and the first of the two gas giants. It has a deep, cold atmosphere, rings, and many moons.

Four of Jupiter's moons are much larger than the rest and can be seen easily from Earth with binoculars or a small telescope. They were discovered by Galileo in 1609 and are called the Galilean moons in his honor.

JUPITER FACTS

Discoverer
Unknown

Discovery date
Prehistoric

Average distance from the Sun
484 million mi.
(779 million km)

Year length
11.86 Earth years

Rotation period
9.93 hours

Equatorial radius
44,423 mi. (71,492km)
(11.2 times Earth)

First reached
1973, by *Pioneer 10*

Gravity compared with Earth
253%

Main atmospheric gases
Hydrogen (90%)
Helium (10%)

Number of moons
79

Jupiter overview

Jupiter has a very powerful magnetic field, about 20,000 times stronger than Earth's, and a system of thin, faint rings, made from dust pulled from its inner moons. This giant world has no solid surface: below its atmosphere lies a thick layer of liquid hydrogen and helium, and under that is a layer of hydrogen that behaves like liquid metal.

Great Red Spot

The Great Red Spot is a vast hurricane on Jupiter that is 1.3 times the diameter (width) of Earth, and it has existed for at least 300 years. Since the 1970s, its color has changed from orange to dark brown.

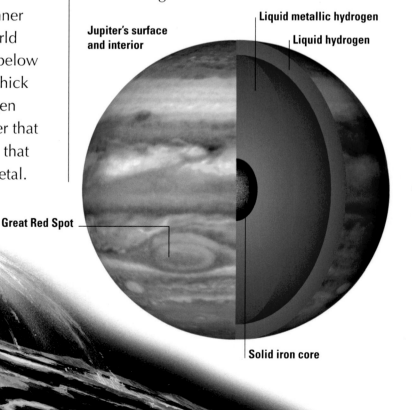

Jupiter's surface and interior

Liquid metallic hydrogen

Liquid hydrogen

Great Red Spot

Solid iron core

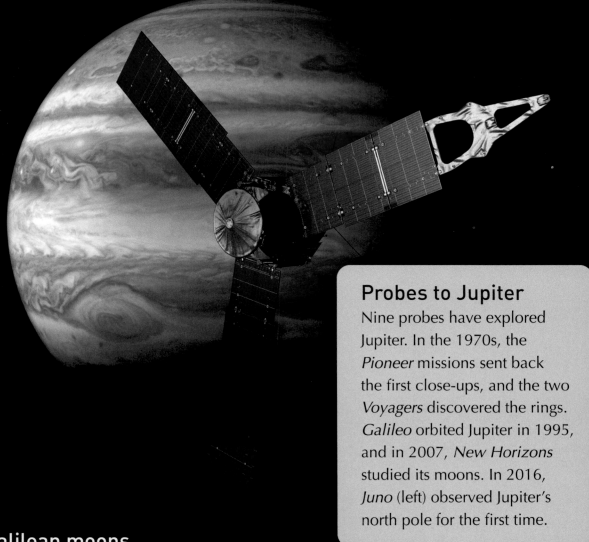

Probes to Jupiter

Nine probes have explored Jupiter. In the 1970s, the *Pioneer* missions sent back the first close-ups, and the two *Voyagers* discovered the rings. *Galileo* orbited Jupiter in 1995, and in 2007, *New Horizons* studied its moons. In 2016, *Juno* (left) observed Jupiter's north pole for the first time.

Galilean moons

Europa and Ganymede

The icy surface of Europa is marked by enormous cracks, and beneath it there is a liquid ocean. Ganymede is made of rock and ice and is the largest moon in the solar system. It is bigger than the planet Mercury.

Io and Callisto

The gravity pulls of Jupiter and Europa produce great heat inside Io, causing volcanoes to erupt there constantly. Callisto, on the other hand, has no volcanoes but is covered in craters formed by the impacts of meteoroids (see p. 60).

Saturn

Saturn is a cold, butterscotch-colored world, ten times farther from the Sun than Earth is. It is the least dense of all of the planets and less dense than water. This means that, if there were an ocean big enough, Saturn would float in it.

Saturn spins on its axis faster than any other planet. This makes its equator bulge outward and flattens it at the poles, so it is more grapefruit- than ball-shaped.

Saturn overview

On Saturn, winds blow ten times faster than a hurricane on Earth. The outer part of the atmosphere is very hazy, which means that the cloud patterns beneath cannot be seen as clearly as those on Jupiter. About every 30 years, huge storms appear. They can be seen as white spots.

Probes to Saturn

Saturn was visited by *Pioneer 11* in 1979 and *Voyagers 1* and *2* in 1980 and 1981. The *Cassini–Huygens* space probe went into orbit around Saturn in 2004 and sent the *Huygens* lander to the surface of Titan.

SATURN FACTS
Discoverer
Unknown
Discovery date
Prehistoric
Average distance from the Sun
890 million mi.
(1,433 million km)
Year length
29.46 Earth years
Rotation period
10.57 hours
Equatorial radius
37,450 mi. (60,270km)
(9.45 times Earth)
First reached
1979, by *Pioneer 11*
Gravity compared with Earth
106%
Main atmospheric gases
Hydrogen (96%)
Helium (3%)
Trace gases (1%)
Number of moons
82

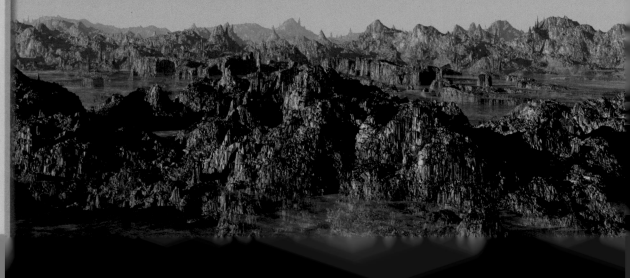

An artist's impression of Titan, with pools containing methane. On Earth, methane is used for fuel.

Saturn's rings

Saturn's rings are the most massive and widest in the solar system. They are made of lumps of dirty ice, from tiny fragments to pieces many feet across. The rings are hundreds of thousands of miles across, yet only a few feet thick in some places. They may be the remains of a moon destroyed long ago.

Saturn's moons

Most of Saturn's moons were discovered by space probes. It is thought that the outer ones were captured by Saturn's gravity. The gravity pulls of some of the moons make gaps in Saturn's ring system. Saturn's largest moon, Titan, is the only moon in the solar system with a thick atmosphere.

Uranus

Uranus is the first of the two ice giants. It looks like a pale blue ball, with few cloud patterns visible on its surface. Under its thick atmosphere is a layer of frozen gases and a rocky core.

The other planets have magnetic fields with north and south poles that are close to the points (called rotational poles) around which the planets spin. Uranus is very different— its magnetic poles are far from its rotational poles.

URANUS FACTS
Discoverer
William Herschel
Discovery date
March 13, 1781
Average distance from the Sun
1.8 billion mi.
(2.87 billion km)
Year length
84.32 Earth years
Rotation period
17.24 hours
Equatorial radius
15,882 mi. (25,560km)
(four times Earth)
First reached
1986, by *Voyager 2*
Gravity compared with Earth
89%
Main atmospheric gases
Hydrogen (about 83%)
Helium (about 15%)
Methane (about 2%)
Number of moons
27

Uranus overview

Uranus is about twice as far from the Sun as Saturn and 19 times as far as Earth. It receives little of the Sun's light and heat, making it a very cold place. Each of the farthest four planets in the solar system make some of their own heat, but Uranus makes much less than the others. This means that it does not have the dramatic weather that the other giant planets do.

Probes to Uranus

Only one probe has visited Uranus: *Voyager 2*, in 1986. It took nine years to reach Uranus and passed within 51,000 mi. (82,000km) of the planet. It studied the atmosphere of Uranus, its largest moons, strange magnetic field, and rings before continuing its journey to Neptune.

The moons of Uranus

Ten of Uranus's moons were discovered by *Voyager 2*, and all of them are named after characters in the plays of William Shakespeare or the poems of Alexander Pope. Miranda, the fifth-largest moon, has a strange, jumbled surface—it is possible that it may have shattered millions of years ago and been pulled together again by gravity.

The rings of Uranus

Nine of Uranus's rings were discovered in 1977 when they caused light from a star behind them to flicker as the rings passed in front of it. Two more rings were found by *Voyager 2* and the rest by the Hubble Space Telescope.

Sideways spin

As Uranus moves around the Sun, its axis points almost directly at the Sun. When it does, days and nights there can sometimes each last for more than 40 years.

ASTRONOMER

DISCOVERY OF URANUS

Uranus can just barely be seen without a telescope, but it was not identified until 1781, when William Herschel spotted it through his homemade telescope. Herschel wanted to name the object Georgium Sidus (George's Star), in honor of Great Britain's King George III, but astronomers from other countries objected, and it was named after a Greek god of the sky, Ouranos. Uranus was the first planet to be discovered since ancient times.

Neptune

Neptune is the most distant planet from the Sun. This means that it has the longest year of all. From Neptune, the Sun looks like a bright star, and the planet receives little heat from it.

Neptune has a deep, very cold atmosphere. It is so similar to that of Uranus that it is puzzling that the two planets are different colors. Underneath there is a thick, icy layer, with a small rocky core in the center.

NEPTUNE FACTS

Discoverer
Johann Gottfried Galle

Discovery date
September 23, 1846

Average distance from the Sun
2.8 billion mi.
(4.5 billion km)

Year length
164.79 Earth years

Rotation period
16.11 hours

Equatorial radius
15,385 mi. (24,760km)
(3.88 times Earth)

First reached
1989, by *Voyager 2*

Gravity compared with Earth
114%

Main atmospheric gases
Hydrogen (80%)
Helium (19%)
Methane (1%)

Number of moons
14

Exploring Neptune

Only one probe has visited Neptune: *Voyager 2*. It reached the planet in 1989, after a 12-year journey. *Voyager 2* discovered that Neptune is a world of storms and saw strange jets of gas and dust on Neptune's moon Triton. It also studied Neptune's rings and discovered six new moons. Because Neptune is so far away, the radio signals from *Voyager* took four hours to reach Earth.

Neptune's weather

Neptune makes its own heat, and this drives a stormy weather system. It has the highest winds in the solar system, enormous black storm spots, and white, fast-moving clouds.

Neptune's moons

Neptune has one large moon, Triton (right), and 13 smaller ones. Triton has jets of nitrogen gas and dust that soar high up above the surface before being knocked sideways by high-speed winds. Triton was discovered only 17 days after Neptune itself. It was probably not formed near Neptune but was captured by its gravity. The image on the left is an imaginary view from Neptune's tiny moon Proteus, showing the shadow of Triton on Neptune's cloudy face.

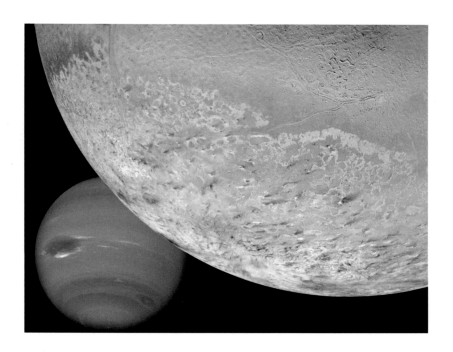

Neptune's rings

Neptune's rings are made of dusty ice particles. They were discovered from Earth in 1984 but were only properly studied by *Voyager 2*, which found that there are five of them. The rings are much thinner in some places than others so that from Earth they look like arcs rather than rings. This may be caused by the gravity of some of Neptune's moons.

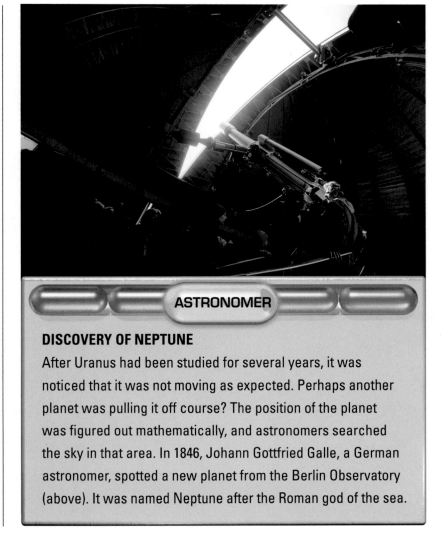

ASTRONOMER

DISCOVERY OF NEPTUNE

After Uranus had been studied for several years, it was noticed that it was not moving as expected. Perhaps another planet was pulling it off course? The position of the planet was figured out mathematically, and astronomers searched the sky in that area. In 1846, Johann Gottfried Galle, a German astronomer, spotted a new planet from the Berlin Observatory (above). It was named Neptune after the Roman god of the sea.

TINY WORLDS

As well as large objects such as the Sun, its planets, and their moons, there are countless smaller worlds that are also members of our solar system.

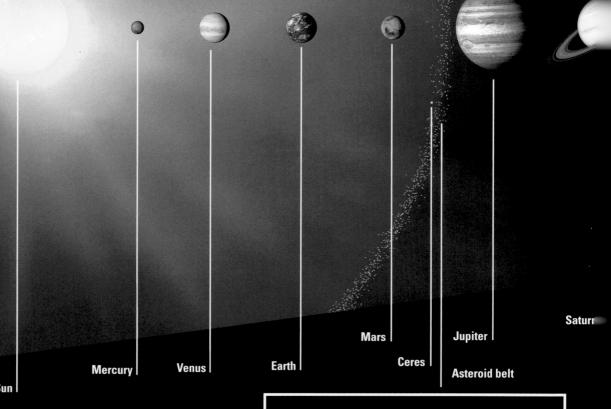

Sun

Mercury

Venus

Earth

Mars

Ceres

Asteroid belt

Jupiter

Saturn

ASTEROIDS

There are billions of lumps of rock or metal called asteroids. Most can be found in the asteroid belt, between Mars and Jupiter. On the right is asteroid Ida, with a tiny asteroid called Dactyl in orbit around it.

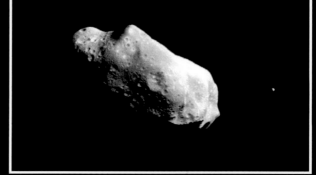

DWARF PLANETS

Dwarf planets are large enough for their gravity to give them rounded or elongated shapes. Only five are known, but there are probably many more that are too small and dim to have been discovered yet. This dwarf planet, Ceres, is the closest to us and the smallest. Haumea, Makemake, and Eris have all been discovered since 2004.

Uranus

Neptune

Pluto

Huamea

Eris

Makemake

Kuiper belt

Oort cloud

KUIPER BELT

The Kuiper belt, a detail of which is shown below, is a ring of cometlike objects. Although 70,000 are more than 60 mi. (100km) across, most are too small to see from Earth. The outer part of the belt is known as the scattered disc.

PLUTO

Until 2006, dwarf planet Pluto was classified as a planet. Made of rock and ice, it has five moons. Pluto's oval orbit means its distance from the Sun changes greatly. The first and only probe to reach Pluto was *New Horizons*, which arrived in 2015.

Space rubble

The solar system is full of dust, grit, and rubble, mostly left over from its formation. At certain times of the year, some of this material can be seen as a faint glow of light in the sky before sunrise or after sunset. This is called the zodiacal light.

Tiny pieces of space dust called micrometeorites drift down constantly to Earth, while larger pieces of falling material can be seen as meteors (shooting stars) as they burn up in the atmosphere.

Uses of meteorites

Before people knew how to obtain metals from rocks, some meteorites were an important source of iron. A large iron meteorite that fell in Greenland about 10,000 years ago was used by the local people for centuries to make tools. Today, meteorites are useful samples of the materials from which the planets formed.

METEORITES

Objects that fall to Earth's surface from space are called meteorites. (They are called meteoroids while they are still in space.) Most meteorites are made of stone, but some are made from iron or a mixture of stone and iron. The largest known meteorite, called Hoba West, weighs about 60 tons.

Meteorites

Impact craters

Many planets, moons, asteroids, and comets are covered in craters caused by meteoroids other asteroids (see p. 58). Large meteorites can also leave craters on Earth. This crater is in Arizona and was caused by an impact about 50,000 years ago.

Meteor Crater in Arizona is more than 0.6 mi. (1km) across.

Down to Earth

As a meteoroid falls through the atmosphere, it squashes the air in front of it, generating so much heat that the meteoroid begins to glow and turns quickly to hot gas and dust. The largest meteors are called fireballs. Sometimes, a fireball can break up on its way through the atmosphere. Some large meteoroids reach the ground before they are destroyed. What is left is called a meteorite.

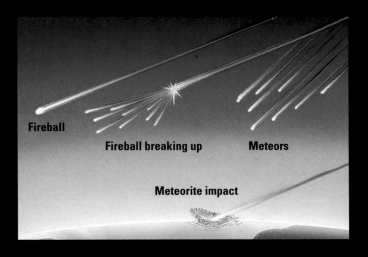

Fireball

Fireball breaking up   Meteors

Meteorite impact

Below: Leonid meteor shower

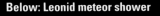

Meteor showers

Some meteoroids are parts of asteroids, while others come from trails of dust and grit left behind by comets. When Earth passes through one of these trails, an entire "shower" of meteors appears. The Leonid shower appears around November 17. It gets its name from Leo, the constellation from where the meteors came.

Comets and the Oort cloud

Comets are visitors from the edge of the solar system, sometimes appearing as misty streaks that glow in the night sky. Comets can last for many nights or weeks before fading away.

Comets are lumps of dirty ice that orbit around the Sun as part of our solar system. As they approach the Sun, some of the ice turns to long trailing tails of gas and dust.

Bluish tail of gas

The misty area around the nucleus is called the coma.

Whitish tail of dust

Tails are often more than 60 million mi. (100 million km) long.

Jupiter impact

In 1994, comet Shoemaker-Levy 9 broke up and many of its fragments crashed onto the planet Jupiter, leaving disturbances in its atmosphere. Jupiter's strong gravity means that it is hit much more often by comets than the other planets are.

Death from space

Astronomers are constantly looking for comets that might pose a risk to Earth. If a large one struck our planet it might cause as much damage as the asteroid which wiped out the dinosaurs sixty-five million years ago.

Oort cloud

Some comets come from an area called the Oort cloud, which is the outermost part of the solar system. Others come from the scattered disk, an area outside the Kuiper belt (see p. 59). Comets start to move toward the Sun from the cloud or disk when they are disturbed by the gravity of other objects. Oort cloud comets are disturbed by passing stars, while it is the outer planets that affect the scattered disk.

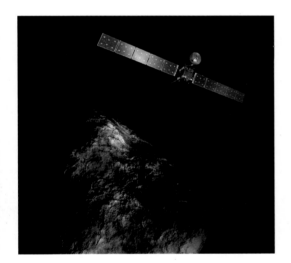

Comet probes

The *Stardust* probe collected dust from the comet Wild 2 in 2004. The probe returned the sample to Earth and went on to visit Tempel 1 in 2011. Tempel 1 had been visited by *Deep Impact* in 2005. The *Rosetta* probe orbited Churyumov–Gerasimenko and sent a lander, *Philae*, to its surface in 2014.

ASTRONOMER

HALLEY'S COMET

Edmond Halley (1656–1742) realized that some comets return regularly to Earth. He studied historical records and predicted that one comet, now named after him, would return in 1758. Sure enough, it did. Since then, records of every visit of Halley's comet have been found, dating back to 240 B.C.

Discovery timeline

Until the telescope was invented in 1609, the planets were seen simply as dots in the sky. But since then, a huge number of discoveries have been made about them and the rest of the solar system.

OBSERVING THE PLANETS

- **1610** Galileo Galilei observes four of Jupiter's moons, the first moons of any other planet to be discovered.
- **1655** Saturn's rings are discovered by Christiaan Huygens.
- **1705** Edmond Halley shows that comets can return many times.
- **1781** Uranus is discovered by William Herschel.
- **1846** Neptune is observed by Johann Gottfried Galle.
- **1930** Pluto, then classed as a planet, is discovered by Clyde Tombaugh.
- **1959** First probe to fly past the Moon: *Luna 1.*
- **1959** Far side of the Moon is seen for the first time by *Luna 3.*

- **1962** First probe to successfully fly past another planet: *Mariner 2.*
- **1965** First probe to reach Mars: *Mariner 4.*
- **1969** First humans land on the Moon: two U.S. astronauts in a lunar module.
- **1970** First rover to explore the Moon: *Lunokhod 1.*
- **1973** First probe to reach Jupiter: *Pioneer 10.*
- **1974** First probe to reach Mercury: *Mariner 10.*
- **1979** First probe to reach Saturn: *Pioneer 11.*
- **1986** First probe to reach Uranus: *Voyager 2.*
- **1986** First probes to reach a comet— Halley's comet: *Vega 1, Vega 2, Giotto, Suisei,* and *Sakigake.*

- **1989** First probe to reach Neptune: *Voyager 2.*
- **1991** First probe to reach an asteroid— 951 Gaspra: *Galileo.*
- **2001** First spacecraft to land on an asteroid—Eros: *NEAR Shoemaker.*
- **2005** *Huygens* becomes the first probe to land on the moon of another planet, Saturn's moon Titan. *Deep Impact* becomes the first probe to make contact with a comet—Tempel 1.
- **2014** First probe to land on a comet— 67P/Churyumov–Gerasimenko: *Philae.*
- **2015** First probe to reach Pluto, *New Horizons.*
- **2018** *Parker Solar Probe* launched on first mission to 'touch' the Sun.

The Sun, eight planets, and our Moon

WEBSITES ABOUT THE SOLAR SYSTEM

http://science.nationalgeographic.com/science/space/solar-system Explore the solar system.

http://starchild.gsfc.nasa.gov/docs/StarChild/solar_system_level1/solar_system.html Solar system facts.

www.jpl.nasa.gov/solar-system/index.cfm Solar system simulator.

STARS
AND GALAXIES

Although the universe is vast and contains trillions of stars, we know a great deal about it. We understand how stars are born and die and why they are found in groups such as clusters and galaxies. But there are still many mysteries to explore and questions to answer.

What is a star?

The thousands of stars that we can see on clear nights are enormous balls of glowing gas, much larger than Earth.

By using a telescope, we can see millions of stars, but there are trillions more that are too far away for us to see at all.

Star types

If a large number of stars are plotted on a graph based on their temperatures (decreasing from left to right across the graph) and their brightnesses (increasing from bottom to top), you get the pattern shown below. The positions of the stars form a diagonal—the main sequence—and a number of groups surrounding it. The main star types can be seen here. Supergiants are enormous and very bright. Giant stars are many times larger than the Sun, which is a main-sequence star. White dwarfs are small and dim.

STELLAR DISTANCES
The distances to the stars can be measured by the time it takes for their light to reach us. Light travels very fast, at 186,282 mi. (299,792km)/sec. It takes less than one-seventh of a second to travel around Earth.

The closest star to us is the Sun, which is 8.1 light-minutes away.

The next-closest star is Proxima Centauri, 4.2 light-years away. It is because the Sun is so much closer than the other stars that it looks so bright. Many of the stars we can see are actually much brighter than the Sun.

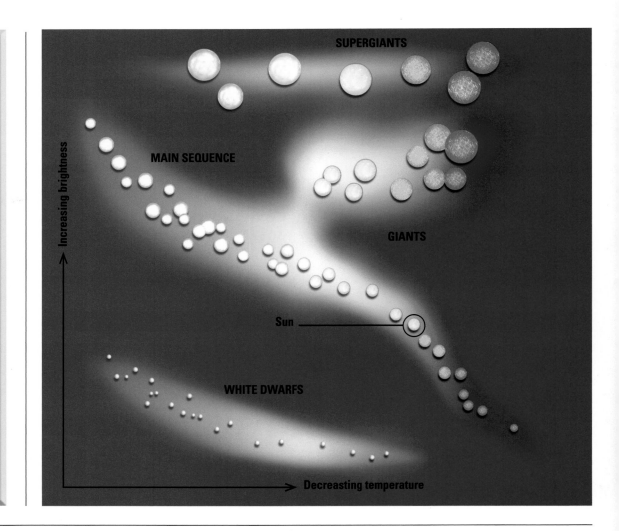

SUPERGIANTS

MAIN SEQUENCE

Increasing brightness

GIANTS

Sun

WHITE DWARFS

Decreasing temperature

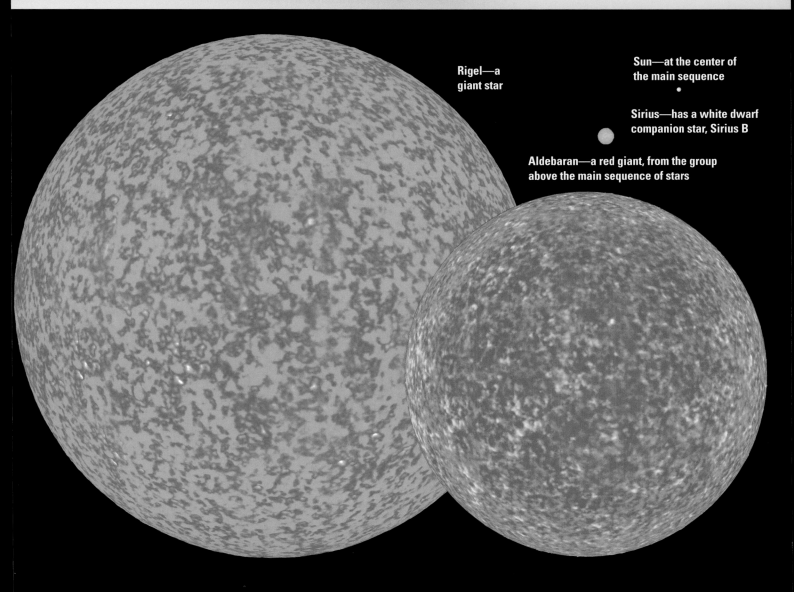

Rigel—a giant star

Sun—at the center of the main sequence

Sirius—has a white dwarf companion star, Sirius B

Aldebaran—a red giant, from the group above the main sequence of stars

The properties of stars

Stars have many different sizes, masses, and brightnesses. The biggest star, discovered in 2010, is about 320 times heavier than the Sun. There are stars more than one million times brighter than the Sun and one that is about 2,000 times wider.

Temperatures and colors

The temperature of a star affects its color. Stars hotter than the Sun are bluish white, while cooler ones are yellow, orange, red, or dark brown. Stars are labeled with letters to show how hot they are. The Sun is a G-type star.

O	B	A	F	G	K	M

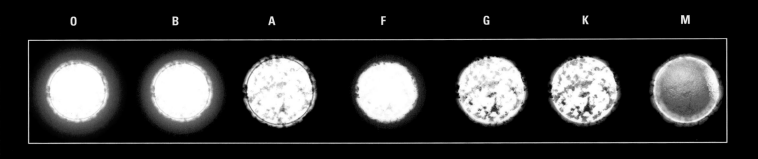

THE SUN

THE GRAVITY OF THE SUN HOLDS THE SOLAR SYSTEM TOGETHER. TO AVOID BEING DRAGGED INTO THE SUN, EARTH AND OTHER PLANETS MUST KEEP MOVING AROUND IT.

TOO BRIGHT TO LOOK AT

The Sun is so bright that you must never look straight at it, because your eyes would be permanently damaged. Even wearing sunglasses is not sufficient protection from the Sun's rays. With a telescope, you can project its image onto a flat sheet of paper and view it safely.

The Sun's brightness means that Earth's surface is light during the day, even when the sky is very cloudy.

SUN FACTS
Mass 2 million trillion trillion tons (330,000 times Earth)
Equatorial radius 432,164 mi. (695,500km) (109 times Earth)
Temperature at center 27 million°F (15 million°C)
Temperature at visible surface about 9,900°F (5,500°C)
Age 4.6 billion years
Gravity at visible surface 28 times Earth
Composition Hydrogen (74%) Helium (25%) Oxygen (1%)

Below: The Sun is so bright that each centimeter of its surface gives out as much light as 250,000 candles.

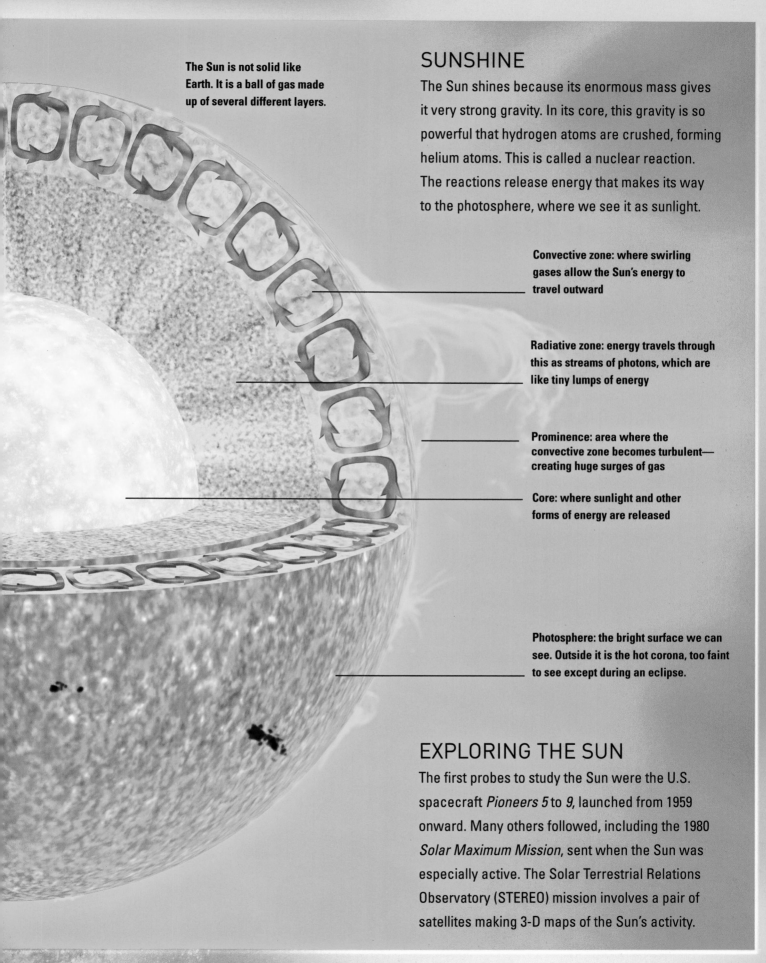

The Sun is not solid like Earth. It is a ball of gas made up of several different layers.

SUNSHINE

The Sun shines because its enormous mass gives it very strong gravity. In its core, this gravity is so powerful that hydrogen atoms are crushed, forming helium atoms. This is called a nuclear reaction. The reactions release energy that makes its way to the photosphere, where we see it as sunlight.

Convective zone: where swirling gases allow the Sun's energy to travel outward

Radiative zone: energy travels through this as streams of photons, which are like tiny lumps of energy

Prominence: area where the convective zone becomes turbulent—creating huge surges of gas

Core: where sunlight and other forms of energy are released

Photosphere: the bright surface we can see. Outside it is the hot corona, too faint to see except during an eclipse.

EXPLORING THE SUN

The first probes to study the Sun were the U.S. spacecraft *Pioneers 5* to *9*, launched from 1959 onward. Many others followed, including the 1980 *Solar Maximum Mission*, sent when the Sun was especially active. The Solar Terrestrial Relations Observatory (STEREO) mission involves a pair of satellites making 3-D maps of the Sun's activity.

The Sun's surface

The surface of the Sun is full of activity, with constantly changing sunspots and other features. This activity increases and decreases over an 11-year period called the solar cycle.

The Sun's very strong magnetic field causes most of the effects that astronomers can see on the Sun's surface.

Solar weather

To describe the activity on the Sun's surface, astronomers use the same terms as meteorologists do for the weather on Earth. They talk about winds and storms on the Sun. Unlike on Earth, solar winds come from the edge of the Sun's atmosphere (corona) and go outward into space, and storms on the Sun happen directly on its surface.

Below: This red prominence is a huge surge of gas. Magnetism lifts it high up above the Sun and can hold it there for hours and even days.

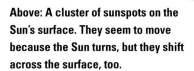

Above: A cluster of sunspots on the Sun's surface. They seem to move because the Sun turns, but they shift across the surface, too.

Sunspots and faculae

Darker areas on the Sun are called sunspots. They are cooler than the surrounding areas and are caused by strong magnetism. Their position varies, and they may last for weeks or months. Bright areas are called faculae. The more sunspots there are, the more faculae there are, too.

Granulation and flares

Granulation is the patchy appearance of the entire surface. Each granule is the top part of an area of convection or gas currents called a cell. Solar flares are huge explosions, while coronal mass ejections are vast bubbles of gas thrown off into space.

A magnetic field joins the two sunspots together.

Sunspots form in pairs, each with an opposite magnetic pole.

Chromosphere

Solar wind particles are thrown off by the sunspots.

Photosphere

Sunspots

The Sun and Earth

A stream of electrically charged particles flows constantly away from the Sun in all directions in the same way that visible light waves stream out. It is called the solar wind and is strongest when the Sun is most active. We cannot see or feel the solar wind, but it does affect Earth by causing the northern and southern lights (also called auroras; see p. 11) and by interfering with radio and television signals.

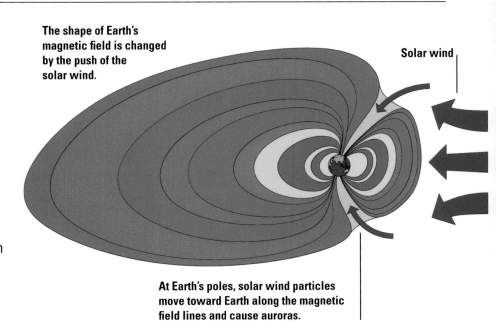

The shape of Earth's magnetic field is changed by the push of the solar wind.

Solar wind

At Earth's poles, solar wind particles move toward Earth along the magnetic field lines and cause auroras.

Star birth

Stars are born, usually in groups, inside dark molecular clouds of dust and gas. Star formation begins when passing stars or supernovae (exploding stars) cause parts of these clouds to collapse.

At several places in a cloud, the material becomes very tightly packed and hot and forms spinning disks. Stars form in the centers of these disks.

Star stories

Because stars last much longer than people, we cannot watch them age. But we can find stars at all stages of their lives and put them in order to understand how they develop. Our knowledge of physics helps us explain this development, and computers are used to see whether these explanations are likely to be correct.

Right: Stars form in the Pillars of Creation, part of the Eagle nebula.

Molecular cloud

A disk begins to form.

Molecular clouds

Molecular clouds are enormous, often hundreds of light-years across. The colder they are, the easier it is to make them collapse and start to form stars. The black areas in the picture are Bok globules, which are thick areas of dust and gas. Some have about the same mass as the Sun. Others are hundreds of times heavier. It is likely that they will turn into spinning disks and then into stars.

T Tauri stars

The spinning disks get very hot in their centers as matter there is squeezed by gravity. Eventually, the centers start to glow and are called protostars. Our sun may have once been a type of protostar called a T Tauri star. The orange star near the center of this image was the first such star to be discovered. T Tauri stars are very active and appear to shine very brightly.

Below: The diagram shows how the Sun was born. A star such as the Sun takes about 50 million years to form from an enormous collapsing molecular cloud.

Star populations

The Sun (right) and many other stars contain a lot of different elements that were formed in older stars and later scattered throughout space. These older stars contained fewer different elements. The newer stars are called Population 2 stars, and the older ones are called Population 1 stars.

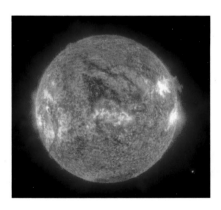

The center of the disk glows, becoming a protostar.

The protostar changes to a true star as nuclear reactions begin.

A young star burns brightly.

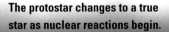

STAR DEATH

How long a star lives depends on its mass—the more massive, the shorter its life will be. The smallest stars last for several hundred billion years. Sunlike stars last for ten billion years, and very massive stars last for just a few million.

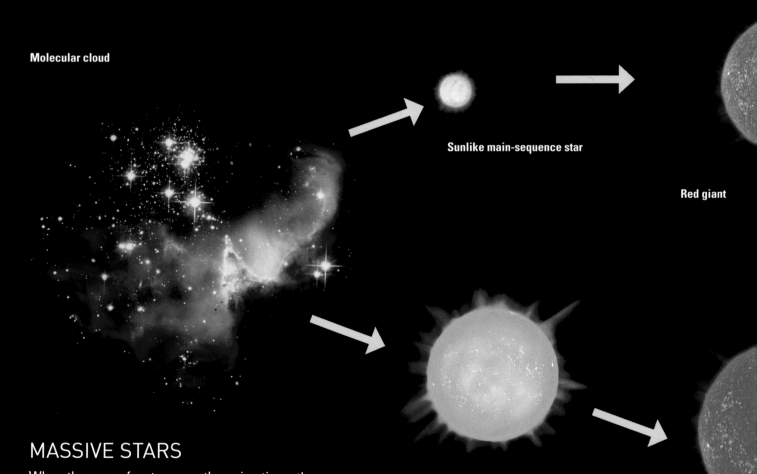

Molecular cloud

Sunlike main-sequence star

Red giant

Massive bright main-sequence star

Red supergiant

MASSIVE STARS

When the core of a star more than nine times the mass of the Sun runs out of hydrogen, the star swells into a red supergiant and uses many other elements as fuel. When all of them run out, the star explodes as a supernova. It leaves behind a neutron star or, if the original star was more than 20 times the mass of the Sun, a black hole.

SUNLIKE STARS

When a Sunlike star runs out of hydrogen in its core, it begins to use helium instead, and swells to form a red giant. Once all of the fuel is exhausted, the star's outer layers are thrown off, forming a huge bubble of gas called a planetary nebula. The star's crushed core remains as a white dwarf, cooling gradually until it turns into a black dwarf.

SUPERNOVAE

Supernova explosions are enormous, often brighter than all of the other stars in a galaxy put together. Unlike the other stages in a star's life, which last for many millions of years, a supernova lasts for only a few days. The elements that were made by the star are scattered throughout space by the supernova. They form part of new stars and planets—and you, too. Another type of supernova is caused by the transfer of material from one star in a binary to the other (see pp. 82–83).

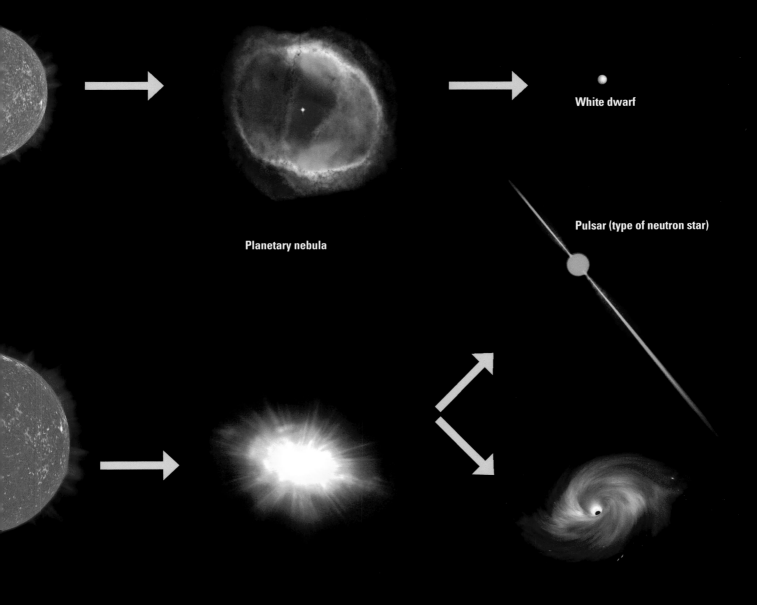

White dwarf

Planetary nebula

Pulsar (type of neutron star)

Supernova

Black hole

Neutron stars and pulsars

While a star is shining, the light and other energy streaming from it tries to make it swell. At the same time, its gravity tries to make it shrink. Usually, the two forces are in balance, which keeps the star from exploding.

When a star runs out of fuel and stops shining, its gravity shrinks it into a much smaller object. Stars like the Sun shrink to white dwarfs, but larger ones shrink even further and become neutron stars.

The Crab nebula

In A.D. 1054, Chinese astronomers saw a new star that was so bright that it could be seen in daylight. They called it a guest star, but we now know it was a supernova. The image shown right is what that area looks like now. It is called the Crab nebula—a vast area of glowing gas that is getting larger all the time. Deep inside it is a pulsar.

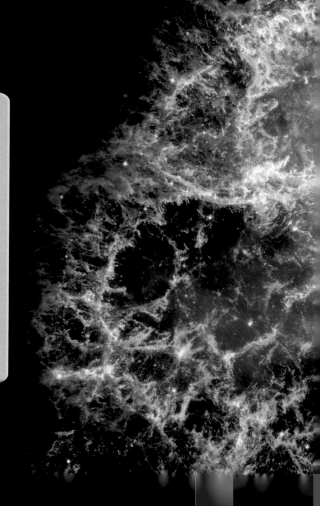

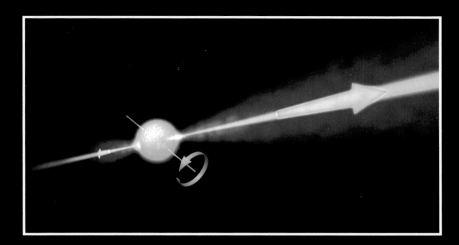

How pulsars work

Neutron stars have strong magnetic fields, and they spin fast. These magnetic fields send narrow streams of radio waves around space. If the radio waves pass across Earth, they can be detected as beeps by radio telescopes. The neutron star is then called a pulsar. As they grow older and run out of energy, the beeps slow down. The Crab pulsar signal is slowing by about one hundred-thousandth of a second per year.

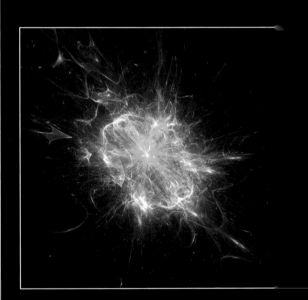

Neutron stars

Neutron stars are only a few miles across, even though they weigh more than the Sun. They are covered in layers of iron. Their strong gravity means that their atmospheres are only a few inches thick. Neutron stars are the dead remains of stars from nine to 20 times the mass of the Sun. Stars that are even more massive form black holes (see p. 79).

BLACK HOLES

IF ENOUGH MATTER IS SQUEEZED INTO A SMALL ENOUGH SPACE, THE GRAVITY IS SO STRONG THAT NOTHING, NOT EVEN LIGHT, CAN ESCAPE. SO THE OBJECT IS BLACK—A BLACK HOLE.

HOW ARE BLACK HOLES SEEN?

Because they are black, only the effects of black holes can be seen. Each is surrounded by a disk of material that gradually falls into it. This material releases energy as it does so, including powerful x-rays. The gravity of black holes can also bend the light from other stars. Both effects can be detected from Earth.

Below: The first ever photograph of a black hole taken by the Event Horizon Telescope in 2019. It is located in a distant galaxy called M87 and is 24.9 billion miles (40 bil. km) across.

Some people think that black holes may one day allow spacecraft to travel great distances across the universe—or even through time.

DISCOVERING BLACK HOLES

The idea of a black hole was first suggested in 1783. In the early 1900s, Albert Einstein's work showed what they might be like, but no one really believed in them until a strong x-ray source called Cygnus X-1 was discovered. It is almost certainly a black hole.

If a spacecraft flew too close to a black hole, it would "spaghettify" as the gravity tore it apart.

SUPERMASSIVE BLACK HOLES

Not all black holes are the remains of dead stars. There are also supermassive black holes in the centers of galaxies. These may be more than one billion times the mass of the Sun. It is thought that they may grow from smaller black holes that draw in extra material, or they may form from collapsing gas clouds.

Variable stars

Not all stars shine steadily. Some vary in brightness over hours, days, months, or years. These stars are called variables. Those that change in a predictable way are called regular variables. Irregular variables are not predictable.

Stars can vary because they change size or because a dust cloud or another star gets in the way of their light. For others, there are sudden enormous explosions.

VARIABLE STARS

Eruptive
Includes R Coronae Borealis stars, which produce sooty clouds, and flare stars

Pulsating
Includes Miras—named after the first variable to be discovered (in 1596), and Cepheids

Rotating
Pulsars, for example

Cataclysmic
Includes novae and supernovae

Eclipsing
Where binary stars pass across one another as seen from Earth

Star shells
The star at the center of this image—V838 Monocerotis—is surrounded by dust shells. In 2002, a series of photos was taken of the star, which had released a huge flare of light. As the light traveled from one dust shell to another, each lit up in turn (as shown in the four images on the right). No such outburst has been seen in any other star, and its cause is uncertain, but it was extremely powerful, making the star about a million times brighter than the Sun. The star itself is enormous—more than 1,000 times as big as the Sun.

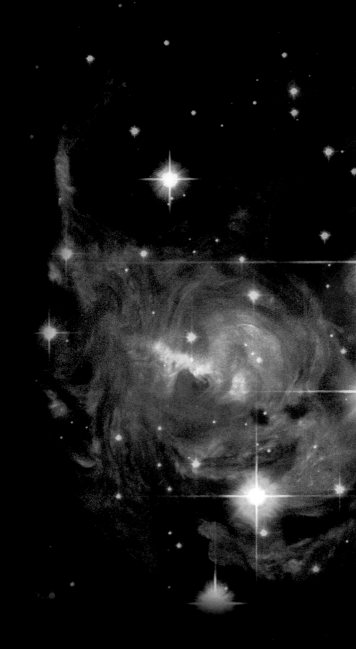

Spotted stars

The Sun usually has many small spots on its surface. But some supergiant stars, such as XX Trianguli (left), have spots so enormous that they cover one-fourth of their surface—or even more. This makes one side darker. Like all stars, XX Trianguli spins, so its brightness changes as seen from Earth. Like the Sun's spots, this one is probably caused by magnetic fields. It is about 1,800°F (1,000°C) cooler than the rest of the star's surface.

Cepheids

A Cepheid's period (the time it takes to vary) depends on how bright it is on average: brighter Cepheids have longer periods. This means that astronomers can determine the true brightness of a Cepheid by measuring its period. By comparing this with how bright it looks, its distance from Earth can be figured out.

Monocerotis

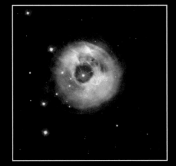

May 20, 2002

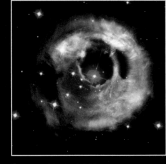

September 2, 2002

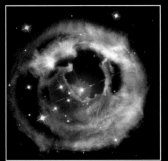

October 28, 2002

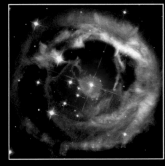

December 17, 2002

BINARY STARS

UNLIKE THE SUN, MOST OF THE STARS IN THE SKY
EXIST IN PAIRS. THESE STARS ARE CALLED BINARIES,
OR DOUBLE STARS. USUALLY, THEY FORMED CLOSE
TOGETHER, AS PART OF THE SAME CLOUD.

A BINARY STAR SYSTEM

In a binary, the stars move around each other. If (as
seen from Earth), they pass in front of each other, the
binary changes in brightness and is called an eclipsing
binary. If the stars are very close, they look like one star,
but astronomers can measure the "wobbles" or color
changes caused by their motion. Binary stars are very
useful because their masses can be determined from
such measurements.

BINARY ORBITS

In a binary, how fast stars orbit each other
depends on their masses and distances apart.
The stars in close binaries orbit in a few days,
but the most widely separated ones take
hundreds of years to go around each other.

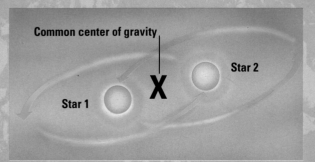

Common center of gravity

Star 2

X

Star 1

CONTACT BINARIES

In a contact binary, the stars are so close that the gravity of each pulls at the atmosphere of the other until the stars actually touch and mix. The stars often get in the way of each other as seen from Earth. This type of eclipsing binary is called a W Ursae Majoris variable.

Some binary stars may have planets moving around them. The temperatures on the surfaces of these planets would change greatly as the planets move away from and toward each star, so it is unlikely that there are living things there.

Star clusters

When many stars form from the same cloud, they often stay together for many millions of years as a star cluster. There are two types of clusters: globular clusters, which are roundish, and open clusters, which are scattered.

Globular clusters contain between several thousand and several million stars. From Earth, they look like misty balls of light. Open clusters contain dozens to thousands of stars.

The Pleiades

The Pleiades open cluster (below) is easy to see from Earth because it is only about 440 light-years away. It is also called the Seven Sisters because it contains seven bright stars (six in view here), as well as many dimmer ones. The Pleiades stars look fuzzy because they are passing through a dust cloud.

CLUSTER NUMBERS
Clusters of stars are common. There are probably about 10,000 open clusters in the Milky Way. They are found in some other galaxies, too, but only if stars are still forming there. There are probably fewer than 200 globular clusters in the Milky Way, but they are found in all large galaxies.

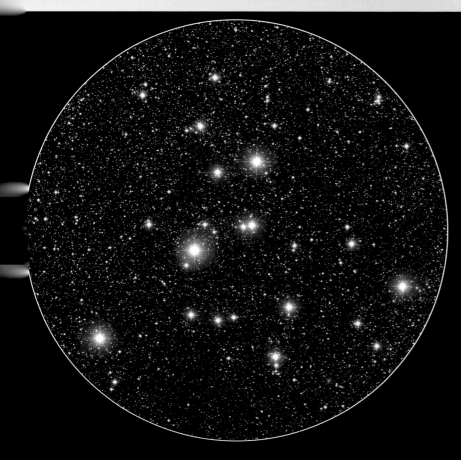

Open cluster

Stars in open clusters drift away over periods of hundreds of millions of years. However, because they are still surrounded by the material from which they were made, the stars that are lost are sometimes replaced by new ones. This cluster is called M39. The "M" stands for Messier, the name of the French astronomer Charles Messier, who discovered it in 1764. M39 is about 800 light-years away from Earth and is between 200 to 300 million years old—much younger than the Sun. M39 is in the constellation of Cygnus, the Swan.

Globular cluster

Globular clusters also drift apart, but their stronger gravity means that this process takes much longer than it does for open clusters, and they can last for billions of years. However, unlike open clusters, globulars never form new stars. This is M13. It is about 150 light-years across and is about 25,000 light-years from us. It contains several hundred thousand stars. On a very dark, clear night, M13 can just barely be seen with the naked eye. Because Messier's telescope was not of good enough optical quality to see details in it clearly, he described M13 as "a nebula containing no stars."

SPACE CLOUDS

SPACE CONTAINS GAS ATOMS AND DUST PARTICLES. IN MOST PLACES, THEY ARE FAR APART, BUT SOMETIMES THEY ARE GATHERED TOGETHER TO FORM CLOUDLIKE OBJECTS CALLED NEBULAE.

TYPES OF NEBULAE

Where dust is thick and cold, it forms black clouds called dark nebulae, such as the Horsehead nebula, shown right. Where oxygen gas is heated by a nearby star, it glows red, forming an emission nebula. Dying stars make bubbles of gas called planetary nebulae, while supernovae leave behind nebulae called supernova remnants.

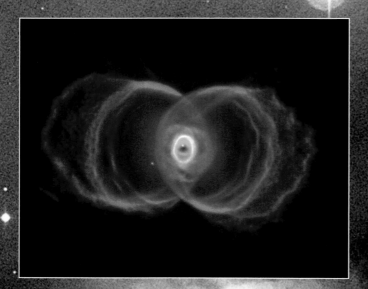

HOURGLASS NEBULA

The Hourglass nebula (above) is an example of a planetary nebula: a bubble of gas thrown out by a dying star. While some planetary nebulae are round, the Hourglass has an odd shape, perhaps because its star has an unusual stellar wind.

PENCIL NEBULA

The Pencil nebula is part of the Vela supernova remnant. It appears as a long, thin band, like a pencil in the sky. It is moving at about 400,000 mph (644,000km/h). It was formed by a supernova about 12,000 years ago and is about 800 light-years away.

ORION NEBULA

The Orion nebula (above) is one of the easiest to see and is a well-photographed object in the night sky. It is about 24 light-years across. In it, new stars and planets are forming from collapsing areas, just as the Sun and Earth did.

The Milky Way

On a clear night with no Moon, you might see a fuzzy band stretching across the sky. This band is called the Milky Way. Through a telescope, it can be seen as millions of stars.

The entire Milky Way, also known as the Galaxy, contains at least 200 billion stars. It is a flattish disk about 100,000 light-years across.

Spiral arms

The Milky Way has several bright spiral arms. They are bright because they contain many young stars that send out a lot of light.

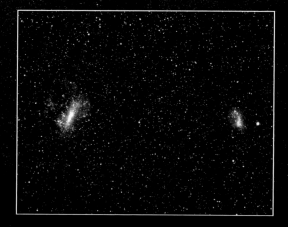

Discovering the Milky Way

Although some ancient Greeks thought that the Milky Way might be made of stars, this was not proved until Galileo Galilei looked at it through a telescope for the first time, in 1609. In 1785, William Herschel made a map of our galaxy and decided that Earth was not far from its center. We now know that his map showed only a very small part of the Milky Way. It was only in the 1920s that all astronomers agreed that the Milky Way is just one of many galaxies.

Magellanic Clouds

In the night skies of the Southern Hemisphere, there are two patches of light that look similar to the Milky Way. They are small galaxies called the Large and Small Magellanic clouds. The gravity of the Milky Way has given them twisted shapes.

Where are we?

The solar system is close to the inner edge of the Orion arm of the Milky Way. It is about two thirds of the way (25,000 light-years) from the center of the Milky Way. The solar system is moving around the Milky Way at the very high speed of around 125 mi. (200km)/sec. Even so, because it has to travel the enormous distance of 160,000 light-years, it takes about 240 million years to go around just once. The Sun and some nearby stars are inside an area called the Local Bubble, where the gas that is found throughout the Milky Way is unusually thin.

The view from Earth

The Milky Way is easier to see from the Southern Hemisphere because from there we are looking toward the bright center of the Galaxy. The darker patches within the Milky Way are dusty areas.

MEDIA

GALACTIC EMPIRES: The *Star Trek* series of television shows and movies follows the interstellar adventures of the exploration vessel the starship *Enterprise*. Here, the USS *Enterprise* (shown above) prevents war breaking out in the Milky Way between two galactic enemies, the Federation and the Klingon Empire.

Galaxies

There are billions of galaxies scattered throughout the known universe. Each is held together by gravity and contains many stars.

Galaxies may contain trillions of stars. Most are small and irregular in shape. It is not certain why this is, nor exactly how galaxies form.

Types of galaxies

There are four types of galaxies, each with a different shape. Some galaxies have no obvious shape (1) and are called irregulars. Elliptical galaxies are shaped like flattened or squashed balls (2). Spiral galaxies have curved arms. The Milky Way is a spiral galaxy and probably has a bar of stars in the middle (3). Some spiral galaxies do not have bars (4).

A spiral galaxy

This a face-on view of the Whirlpool galaxy. It is a typical spiral galaxy, with a bright central bulge and spiraling arms of stars. The galaxy is constantly spinning, forming a pattern similar to a whirlpool or water spiraling down a drain. The bulge is a dense mass of old stars. The wispy arms are areas rich in young stars and glowing gas. Galaxies like this one are fairly rare.

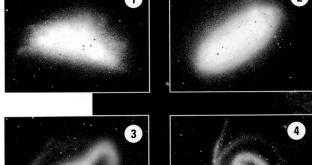

Colliding galaxies

These two galaxies are called the Mice. They have strange shapes because they are in the process of colliding. The gravity of each galaxy pulls the other out of shape and also causes the birth of hundreds of new stars each year.

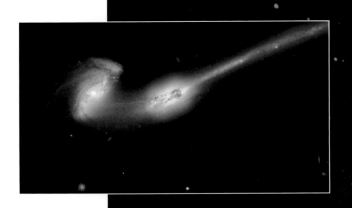

Energy given off

Black hole

Matter spins around as it is drawn in.

Active galaxies

Active galaxies contain enormous black holes. Matter falling into the holes sends out huge amounts of radiation (above). Active galaxies look very different depending on the angle we see them from. If we see them between face-on and edge-on, they are called quasars. Quasars are among the brightest and most distant light sources we know.

THE UNIVERSE

THE UNIVERSE IS EVERYTHING THAT EXISTS. WE DO NOT KNOW HOW LARGE THE UNIVERSE IS, BECAUSE WE CAN SEE ONLY AS FAR AS A FEW BILLION LIGHT-YEARS. THIS AREA IS CALLED THE KNOWN UNIVERSE. MOST OF IT IS COLD AND EMPTY.

BEYOND THE STARS

If you could travel away from Earth at an amazing speed, you would soon leave the Moon behind and then all of the planets. You would pass many stars, but eventually these would thin out, because you would have left the Milky Way galaxy. Outside it, you would see many other galaxies, clustered together in groups of many sizes (called clusters and superclusters). Traveling even farther, you would see that these clusters and superclusters form long strands (called filaments), with empty spaces between them.

Milky Way
Our galaxy, the Milky Way, is about 100,000 light-years across and more than 2,000 light-years thick.

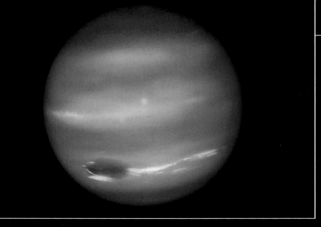

Earth and the Moon
The Moon is Earth's closest neighbor. It is about 1.3 light-seconds away.

Planets in the solar system
The distance from the Sun to Neptune is about 4.2 light-hours. The outer edge of the Oort cloud may be more than one light-year away.

AN ENDLESS SPACE

The universe has no center and no edges. It is not known if the universe is infinite (goes on forever) or finite (limited in volume). Even if it is finite, you could never reach the end of the universe. This is a little like Earth: although you could travel on it forever without reaching an end, it has only a limited area to explore.

Local Group
The Milky Way is part of the Local Group of galaxies. There are about 30 others, most much smaller than the Milky Way. This is the Andromeda galaxy, M31.

Distant galaxies
Many galaxies can be seen here. Galaxies are found in clusters—like the Local Group—that are themselves grouped into superclusters. Groups of superclusters form vast filaments, with enormous empty regions between them.

The big bang

The universe began billions of years ago as a colossal burst of energy. Instantly, it began to expand, and all the groups of galaxies are still moving apart, as the expansion continues.

Ever since the universe began, it has been expanding at incredible speed. It was formed 13.7 billion years ago in a sudden burst of energy called the big bang.

Cosmic background radiation

Although the idea of the big bang was suggested in 1925, many astronomers doubted it until the leftover heat radiation from the big bang was measured in 1964. This is called cosmic microwave background radiation. Measurements of variations in the radiation allow astronomers to trace the beginning of galaxies in the early universe.

The big bang

The big bang was the beginning of everything— even time and space. It was a sudden and mysterious burst of energy and was extremely hot. Very soon after the big bang, there was a short period of very fast expansion called cosmic inflation. Since then, the universe has continued to expand and cool down.

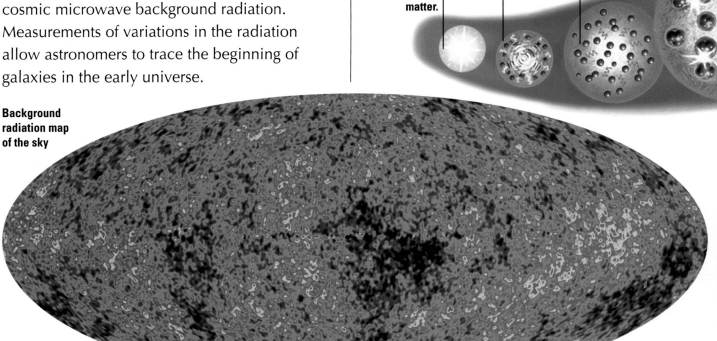

Sudden burst of energy. At this stage, the universe contains no matter.

The simplest particles start to form.

The universe contains quarks and gluons.

Quarks and gluons form larger particles.

Background radiation map of the sky

Blue areas are high in radiation; yellow areas are low in radiation.

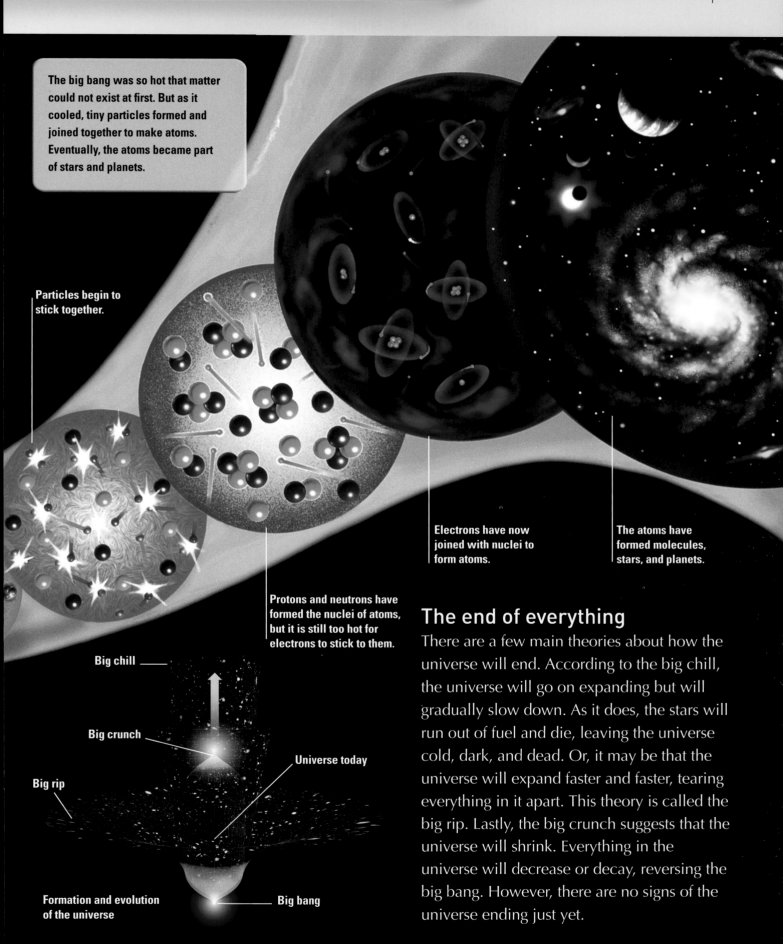

The big bang was so hot that matter could not exist at first. But as it cooled, tiny particles formed and joined together to make atoms. Eventually, the atoms became part of stars and planets.

Particles begin to stick together.

Electrons have now joined with nuclei to form atoms.

The atoms have formed molecules, stars, and planets.

Protons and neutrons have formed the nuclei of atoms, but it is still too hot for electrons to stick to them.

Big chill

Big crunch

Universe today

Big rip

Formation and evolution of the universe

Big bang

The end of everything

There are a few main theories about how the universe will end. According to the big chill, the universe will go on expanding but will gradually slow down. As it does, the stars will run out of fuel and die, leaving the universe cold, dark, and dead. Or, it may be that the universe will expand faster and faster, tearing everything in it apart. This theory is called the big rip. Lastly, the big crunch suggests that the universe will shrink. Everything in the universe will decrease or decay, reversing the big bang. However, there are no signs of the universe ending just yet.

Space distances

One of the most difficult and important parts of astronomy is finding out how large the universe is and how far away the things in it are from one another. There are different methods of measurement for different types of objects.

SOLAR SYSTEM DISTANCES

The distance to the Moon is measured by bouncing laser beams off it and timing how long it takes for them to come back. This is about 2.6 seconds, which means that the Moon is about 1.3 light-seconds away. The same method is used to measure the distances to the planets, except that radio waves are used instead of light. This is how we know that Venus, the closest planet to us, is about 25 million mi. (40 million km, or about 2.2 light-minutes) away at its closest. Planetary distances are also often measured in astronomical units: Earth is about one astronomical unit from the Sun.

STAR DISTANCES

Stars are very far from Earth. It is impractical to measure the distance of stars in miles or kilometers because those numbers would be too big. Instead, astronomers use light years to measure how far away stars are. A light year is the distance a ray of light travels in a year, which is about 6 trillion miles (9 trillion kilometers). Starlight takes many years to reach Earth, with Earth's closest star being 4.3 light years away. Astronomers who study far away galaxies measure distances from stars in parsecs: one parsec is 3.26 light years

GALACTIC DISTANCES

Galaxies are light-centuries away. They contain variable stars, such as the Cepheids, and the brightnesses and distances of these can be determined by measuring how fast they change brightness. More distant galaxies can be studied by figuring out their true sizes from their shapes and comparing this with their apparent sizes to determine how far away they are. Also, as we know that distant galaxies are moving away from us, we can figure out their distances from their speeds. Distances to galaxies are often measured in megaparsecs: a megaparsec is one million parsecs.

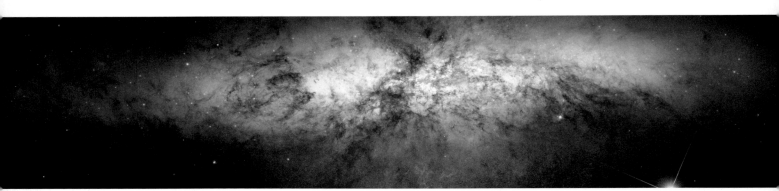

A distant galaxy

WEBSITES ABOUT SPACE AND TIME

http://resources.schoolscience.co.uk/STFC/bang/bang.htm   Travel in time to and from the big bang.

http://spaceplace.nasa.gov/black-hole-rescue Facts, information, and a game about black holes.

www.esa.int/esaKIDSen/Starsandgalaxies.html   Information about stars and the Milky Way.

http://hubblesite.org/explore_astronomy/way_out   Test your knowledge of the universe.

SPACE EXPLORATION

The exploration of space is a vast project, and we are still at the very beginning of it. The only other world that people have traveled to is the Moon. However, space probes have visited every planet and many other objects in the solar system. Space travel needs the best technology and relies on many countries working together.

Space pioneers

People have dreamed of traveling into space for hundreds of years. Usually, the Moon has been their destination. In fact, almost as soon as it was realized that the Moon was another world, people talked about going there.

None of the early writers who dreamed of going to the Moon came up with a practical way of getting there, but their stories did encourage scientists to think about how real spacecraft might work.

Early tales

The earliest story of a journey to the Moon was by a giant waterspout, thought up by a Greek writer named Lucian of Samosata more than 2,000 years ago. He called his story *True History* as a joke, because he knew no one would believe it. In it, the waterspout carries a sailing ship to the Moon, whose inhabitants are at war with the Kingdom of the Sun over the possession of Venus, known as the "Morning Star."

Flying through space

In 1638, the Bishop of Hereford wrote a book called *The Man in the Moone*, in which a flock of geese carry a chair—and an astronaut—to the Moon.

First flight

Robert Goddard (1882–1945) was an American engineer who spent many years figuring out the mathematics of rocket flight. In 1926, he launched the world's first liquid-fueled rocket. Although it flew only for 2.5 seconds, the idea was so good that all later spacecraft were based on it.

Konstantin Tsiolkovsky

Russian engineer Konstantin Tsiolkovsky (1857–1935) was fascinated by the idea of space travel but had little money to carry out experiments. Instead, he worked out many of the basic ideas of space flight and suggested many things that were built decades later, from step rockets (p. 101) to space stations (pp. 120–121). He also determined the speed and fuel that a rocket needs in order to escape from Earth.

MEDIA

FIRST MEN IN THE MOON

In 1901, H. G. Wells wrote *The First Men in the Moon.* In it, an inventor discovers a metal that cuts off gravity and uses it to build a spacecraft. He and a friend travel deep inside the Moon, which turns out to be inhabited and provided with air. The image above is from a 1960 movie of the story.

Escaping gravity

To travel through space, a craft must first escape from Earth, which means overcoming the force of gravity. To do this, the craft must travel upward extremely fast, and the only way we know to do that is by using rocket power.

Rockets fly very differently to planes. Planes rely on air flowing over their wings to lift them off the ground and stay up. For rockets, air causes friction and slows them down: they fly best in the vacuum (airless emptiness) of space.

ESCAPE VELOCITIES

The escape velocity of a rocket depends on the pull of a planet's gravity. This is why the *Apollo* astronauts needed a huge rocket to blast off Earth, with its strong gravity, but a tiny rocket to escape from the Moon, which has much weaker gravity. These escape velocities are in units of mi./sec.

Asteroid Vesta:	0.2
Moon:	1.5
Mars:	3.1
Earth:	7.0
Sun:	383.7

How rockets move

By allowing the gases produced from burning fuel to escape through the back of a rocket's combustion chamber, a forward force called thrust is created.

NASA

Escape velocity

The harder you throw a stone upward, the higher it gets before falling. If you could throw it hard enough, it would never come down again but would continue into space. The speed necessary for this is the escape velocity.

Reusable rockets

For a long time, rockets could only be used once. Step rockets would discard their fuel tanks on their way into space and a new rocket would be built for each mission. In recent years this has changed and new rockets, such as the Falcon rockets built by SpaceX, are designed to be almost completely reusable. These rockets deliver their payloads in space, then turn around and land back on Earth. They are then cleaned, refuelled, and used again.

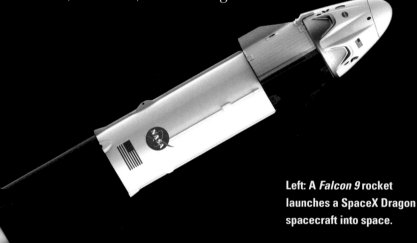

Left: A *Falcon 9* rocket launches a SpaceX Dragon spacecraft into space.

Above: The reusable first stage of a SpaceX *Falcon 9* rocket is recovered, ready to refurbish and refuel for the next launch.

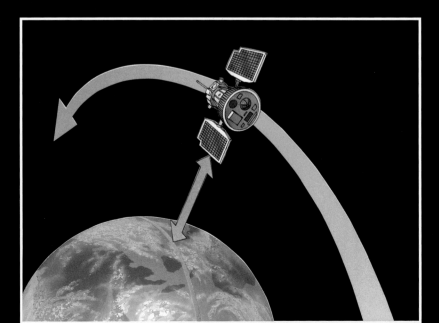

Orbital velocity

It is not necessary to completely escape from Earth's gravity if a spacecraft needs only to reach the Moon or to go into orbit. In fact, no rocket carrying people has ever reached escape velocity. The velocity needed to reach orbit and stay there is known as the orbital velocity. It depends on the size of the orbit, but for Earth it is around 4 mi. (7km)/sec.

Traveling through space

Almost all of the fuel carried by a spacecraft is used up within a few minutes of launch in order to move it away from Earth and send it on its way.

Once it is beyond the atmosphere and going fast enough, a rocket does not need to keep firing its engines to continue moving. It will stop only if it is pulled down by the gravity of a planet or other large object.

The first stage of this rocket consists of four boosters, each about 66 ft. (20m) long. These burn fuel for the first two minutes of a flight, creating the thrust needed to propel the rocket up into the air. The boosters then fall away from the rocket. As the used stages fall back to Earth, they burn up in the atmosphere.

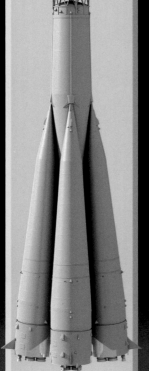

SOYUZ ROCKET
The Russian *Soyuz* rocket is used to lift military and civilian payloads into space. It is the most frequently used launch craft in the world. Its main fuel is kerosene.

Types of fuel
Rocket fuel is either liquid or solid. Hydrogen is a common liquid rocket fuel and powdered aluminum a solid rocket fuel. As there is no air in space, rockets need to take oxygen with them. Without it, the fuel would not burn.

The second stage of *Soyuz* burns fuel for another two and a half minutes and then separates from the last stage.

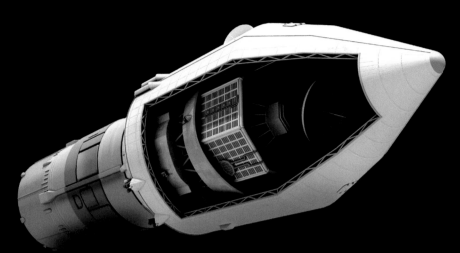

Payloads

A rocket's payload is whatever it is designed to carry—such as a crewed capsule or a satellite. Spacecraft are the most expensive way to travel—while a truck can easily carry a load greater than its own weight, a rocket may be 40 times as heavy as its payload.

The third stage burns fuel for another six minutes and then opens its shroud to release the payload.

The fourth stage delivers the payload into orbit. Here, the payload is a communication satellite.

Slingshots

Space probes to distant parts of the solar system use the gravity of planets to help them on their way. This is known as a gravitational slingshot effect, and it both speeds up the space probes and changes their directions.

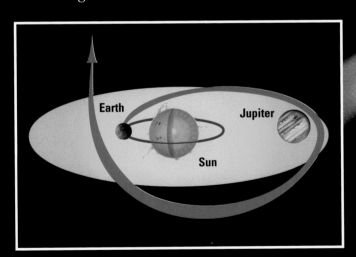

Earth

Jupiter

Sun

Steering a spacecraft

To steer a rocket on its way up into space, its engine nozzle can be "gimbaled"—that is, pointed slightly to one side. Once in space, small rockets or compressed air jets are used to change direction.

THE SPACE RACE

On October 4, 1957, *Sputnik 1*, the first artificial satellite, was launched by the U.S.S.R. It was the start of a space race between the U.S.S.R. and the U.S.

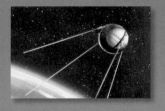

Sputnik 1 sent out a beeping radio signal that could be heard around the world.

Gagarin in his capsule

Cutaway of Gagarin's *Vostok 1* capsule, called *Swallow*. Only the spherical reentry capsule of the craft returned to Earth.

YURI GAGARIN

The first human in space was Yuri Gagarin, a 27-year-old Russian air-force pilot. Gagarin was chosen partly because of his small size—the capsule had very little room. He went around Earth once in his capsule on April 12, 1961. Gagarin bailed out of the capsule on the way down, landing by parachute. He immediately became an international hero.

JOHN GLENN

The U.S. was determined to catch up with the U.S.S.R. It succeeded in putting an American named John Glenn into orbit the year after Gagarin. Glenn completed three orbits of Earth in his capsule. He returned to space on the space shuttle 36 years later. Then aged 77, he became the world's oldest space traveler.

An *Atlas* rocket launched Glenn into space from Cape Canaveral, Florida.

Glenn's *Mercury* capsule was called *Friendship 7*. After a flight lasting almost five hours, it splashed down into the Atlantic Ocean.

Gagarin's space trip began with the blastoff of the *Vostok-K* rocket from Baikonur Cosmodrome in the U.S.S.R.

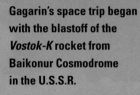

Mission to the Moon

Reaching the Moon was the final aim of the space race—and one of the greatest events in history. Powerful *Saturn V* rockets carried *Apollo* modules with astronauts onboard.

MOON MODULES

The three *Apollo* astronauts in each crew traveled to the Moon's orbit and back in the command module (CM), with the service module (SM) attached. Two of the astronauts traveled between the CM and the Moon's surface in the lunar module (LM).

The bottom half of *Apollo 11*'s LM, named *Eagle*, was left on the Moon, and the upper part returned to the other modules.

SM

CM

LM

To go to the Moon and back, each of the U.S.'s *Apollo* Moon missions involved traveling more than 430 million mi. (700 million km) through space at record-breaking speeds.

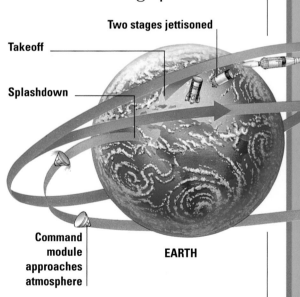

Two stages jettisoned

Takeoff

Splashdown

Command module approaches atmosphere

EARTH

Many missions

Apollo 11 was the first mission to touch down on the Moon, landing on July 16, 1969. Five other *Apollo* landings followed. To prepare the astronauts and test the equipment, a series of practice missions called *Gemini* were made first.

Escape from Earth

Within ten minutes of launch, the first and second stages had been emptied of fuel and cast off. The third stage pushed the modules into Earth's orbit. Another burst from its engines pushed *Apollo* to the Moon.

Third stage and modules head for the Moon

Command module detaches from service module

Return to Earth

After the lunar module had visited the Moon, its upper part rejoined the service module and command module, which were joined together in lunar orbit. Leaving the lunar module and service module in space, only the command module returned to Earth.

Liftoff
At launch, *Saturn V* burned enough fuel every ten seconds to fill a swimming pool. The force of liftoff made the astronauts almost four times heavier than normal during the rockets firing.

On the Moon
The weak lunar gravity meant that the astronauts could easily cope with the bulky space suits that provided them with air and protection. They hopped rather than walked.

Splashdown
The command module had a special heat shield to stop it from burning up as it fell through Earth's atmosphere. Parachutes slowed its fall, and it splashed down in the Pacific.

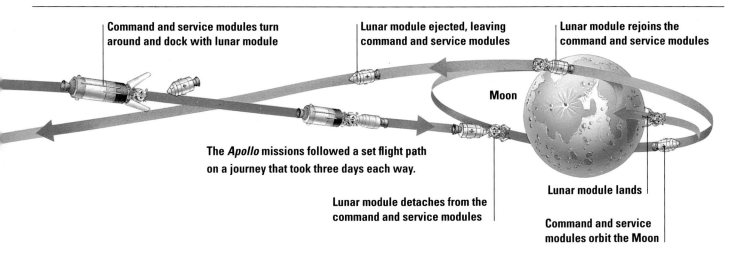

Command and service modules turn around and dock with lunar module

Lunar module ejected, leaving command and service modules

Lunar module rejoins the command and service modules

Moon

The *Apollo* missions followed a set flight path on a journey that took three days each way.

Lunar module detaches from the command and service modules

Lunar module lands

Command and service modules orbit the Moon

Across space
The spacecraft left Earth's atmosphere at 24,100 mph (38,800km/h). Gradually, it slowed down as Earth's gravity tried to pull it back—until it reached the point where the Moon's gravity became stronger, pulling it faster and faster toward the Moon. Except when the engines were firing, the astronauts onboard were weightless and floated around their cabin.

Lunar orbit and landing
Only two of the three-man crews of each *Apollo* mission landed on the Moon. The third crewmate remained in orbit in the linked command and service modules, waiting for the others to return. The first landing was watched on TV by more than one-fifth of the world's population. They heard the now-famous words, "The *Eagle* has landed."

Men on the Moon

Only 12 people—all American men—have walked on the Moon, and no one has set foot there since *Apollo 17* blasted off on December 19, 1972. Partly, this is because of the enormous expense and complexity of the missions.

The Moon missions did more than win the space race for the U.S. They also allowed many new scientific discoveries to be made and taught humans how to travel through space.

Above: *Apollo* mission control in Houston, Texas

Above: Official badge of the first Moon-landing mission

Left: Buzz Aldrin's footprint

First footsteps

Neil Armstrong was the first human to walk on the Moon, on July 20, 1969. Along with Edwin "Buzz" Aldrin, he had landed the lunar module in an area called the Sea of Tranquility. Meanwhile, Michael Collins remained in orbit around the Moon.

Moon experiments

Aldrin and Armstrong had less than two hours to explore their new world. As well as collecting rocks, they carried out several experiments on the Moon. They set up a lunar earthquake detector and a special type of mirror. A laser beam from Earth used the mirror to measure the distance to the Moon to within 2 in. (6cm).

Lunar rovers

Later Moon missions carried electric cars called lunar rovers with them, which meant that their crews could explore much larger areas of the Moon than was possible on foot. The rovers could travel at speeds of up to about 8 mph (13km/h). They were left behind on the Moon.

Precious stones

The rocks collected from the Moon were very valuable, because they helped prove how and when the Moon formed (see p. 44). Pieces were sent to many countries so that scientists could examine them.

The space shuttle

The rockets used to reach the Moon and to put satellites into orbit were costly, and they could be used only once. It was not until the 1980s that reusable spacecraft were developed.

SHUTTLE FLIGHTS
Columbia 28 flights, from 1981 to 2003 (destroyed)
Challenger 10 flights, from 1983 to 1986 (destroyed)
Discovery 39 flights, from 1984 to 2011
Atlantis 33 flights, from 1985 to 2011
Endeavour 25 flights, from 1992 to 2011

Each shuttle consisted of an orbiter, which carried the crew, a large fuel tank, and two booster rockets. Six shuttles were built, although the first was not used for space travel. It was named *Enterprise* after the starship in *Star Trek*.

A reusable spacecraft
Except for the external tank, the shuttle was fully reusable. The twin solid-fuel rocket boosters were discarded when their fuel ran out, but they were fitted with parachutes, so they splashed down undamaged and could then be collected. The external tank burned up as it fell through the atmosphere.

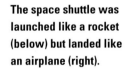
The space shuttle was launched like a rocket (below) but landed like an airplane (right).

Return to Earth
When it had completed its mission, the orbiter was turned around and fired its engines to slow itself down. It dropped down through the atmosphere and landed on a runway, just like a plane. A parachute was used to slow down the orbiter's landing.

Shuttle disasters

In total, space shuttles made 135 space flights. Two of these flights were disasters—in 1986, *Challenger* exploded 73 seconds after launching, killing its crew. The explosion was caused by a fault on one of the solid-fuel rocket boosters. Due to a damaged wing, *Columbia* broke apart on its way back to Earth in 2003. Again, the entire crew was killed.

Shuttle missions

The shuttle was designed to carry out a range of missions, including launching satellites and repairing them, if necessary, and taking astronauts and material to and from *Mir* (see p. 121) and the International Space Station (see pp. 122–123).

The shuttle *Discovery* was used to place the Hubble Space Telescope in orbit in 1990. The telescope was lifted from the shuttle's cargo bay by a robotic arm.

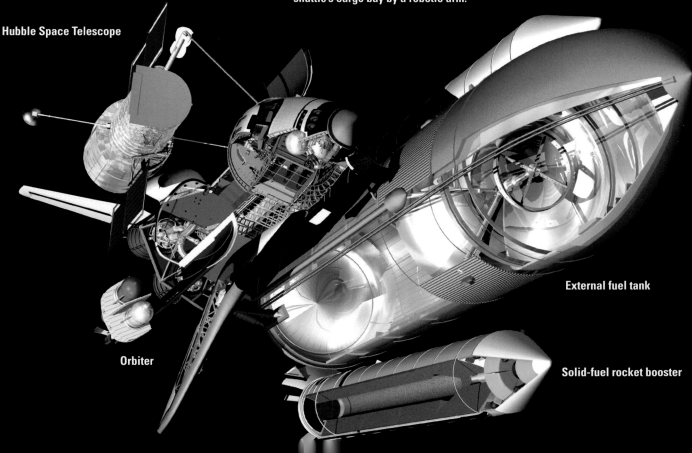

Hubble Space Telescope

External fuel tank

Orbiter

Solid-fuel rocket booster

SPACE SUITS

SPACE SUITS ARE VITAL PIECES OF SURVIVAL EQUIPMENT. THERE ARE TWO MAIN TYPES: ONE IS WORN IN SPACECRAFT DURING LAUNCH AND REENTRY AND THE OTHER IS FOR SPACE WALKS OUTSIDE.

SPACECRAFT SUITS

Launch suits are worn to protect an astronaut in case the cabin loses pressure or needs to be evacuated. During the return to Earth, the suits also squeeze the astronaut's lower body to stop blood from gathering there.

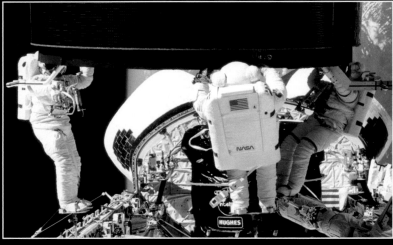

SPACE-WALK SUITS

Any tasks done outside a spacecraft are known as extravehicular activities, or EVAs. EVA suits are like mini spaceships. They provide heat or cooling, together with water, food, and protection against dangerous radiation and the vacuum of space. Waste gases that are breathed out are taken in by the suit and replaced with oxygen to breathe. A urine collector is used as needed.

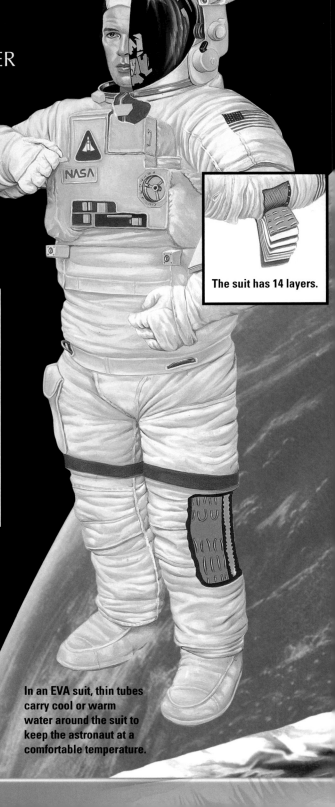

A TV camera and lights are attached next to the astronaut's helmet.

The suit has 14 layers.

In an EVA suit, thin tubes carry cool or warm water around the suit to keep the astronaut at a comfortable temperature.

This EVA space suit, called an extravehicular mobility unit (EMU), was designed for the space shuttle.

An EVA suit also provides radio equipment for communication and instruments that monitor the astronaut's health.

OUTSIDE THE SPACECRAFT

On most EVAs, astronauts are attached to their spacecraft by tethers, and they move by pulling themselves along the craft. But sometimes they must float through empty space. To do this, they use special maneuvering units. The units squirt jets of compressed air that push an astronaut in the opposite direction—just like mini rockets.

Above: An astronaut uses a manned maneuvering unit (MMU) to move around freely in space.

Living in space

The lack of gravity in a spacecraft makes life very different there. Almost every aspect of life is affected, from eating and moving around to going to the bathroom and sleeping.

Training for space

Astronauts need special equipment and training. In training, they can experience weightlessness for brief periods (see right) by traveling in aircraft that swoop down through the air. They also need to learn how to cope with the brief increases in their weight that take place when spacecraft are launched. In orbit—or in a spacecraft that is moving without using its engines—people and other objects are almost weightless. They experience only the tiny gravity of the spaceship itself and small forces owing to changes in speed. These small effects are called microgravity.

Below: In weightless conditions, trainee astronauts float inside a cushioned aircraft fuselage. A technician, with his feet strapped to the floor to stop him from floating, holds a female astronaut horizontal.

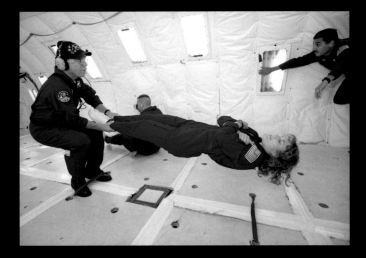

Life in space

In microgravity, everything floats freely, including pens that work upside down. Liquids break into floating droplets that drift around the spacecraft, so drinks must be squeezed into the mouth from special packs. A special toilet sucks away urine and feces. To sleep, astronauts strap themselves to a wall so that they do not drift around.

Space sickness

Many astronauts experience space sickness, which is like carsickness. Luckily, it soon wears off. Other changes in the body take longer. They include the weakening of bones and muscles and the loss of blood cells. As the spine stretches, astronauts get a couple of inches taller, too! Their bodies return to their normal heights and blood-cell counts when the astronauts return to Earth.

Right: Astronaut Chris Hadfield played the guitar in his free time while aboard the International Space Station.

Below: Astronaut Tim Peake wore a harness to keep him on the treadmill as he ran a marathon in space.

Long missions

On long missions, astronauts must cope with the mental pressure of being cooped up with the same few people. It is also vital to exercise, to stop bones and muscles from getting too weak. The longest space flight was made by Valeri Polyakov, who spent 437 days on the *Mir* space station.

Satellites

Any object that moves around a planet or other object in space is a satellite. Earth has one natural satellite, the Moon. It also has many artificial satellites, sent into orbit to do tasks.

SATELLITE ORBITS
Thousands of artificial satellites orbit Earth in one of four paths through space:

Geostationary orbit
Satellite remains constantly over the same part of Earth; used for weather forecasting, communication, and navigation.

Low-Earth orbit
Satellite stays close to Earth; used for cell-phone communication systems.

Polar orbit
Satellite passes over the North and South poles; used for navigation and weather forecasting.

Highly elliptical orbit
Satellite travels in an oval orbit that takes it far from Earth at some points and close at others; used for communication.

An object dropped from high above Earth will fall straight down toward it. But if it is moving sideways fast enough, it will keep going around Earth instead, becoming a satellite.

Escaping the atmosphere
A satellite must orbit at a great enough height to avoid being slowed down by the atmosphere. Satellites can orbit Earth at any distance beyond this height. The farther out they are, the slower they travel.

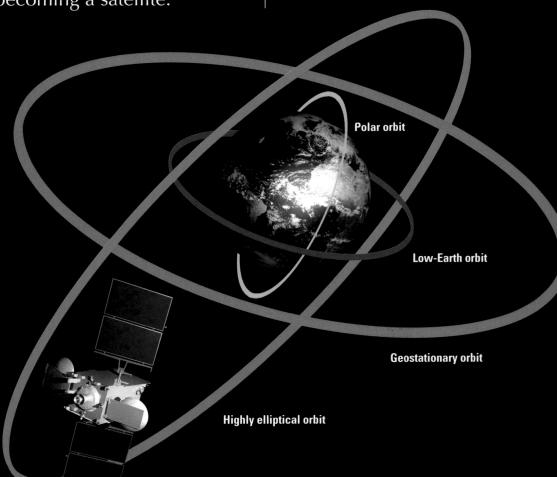

Polar orbit

Low-Earth orbit

Geostationary orbit

Highly elliptical orbit

Communicating with satellites

Satellites communicate by radio signals, which are picked up by dishes (below). Some of the signals provide a satellite's location. Other signals help create photographs or maps of Earth or take measurements of its features.

Launch vehicles

The rockets used to launch satellites into space vary depending on how high a satellite must orbit. More powerful rockets are needed for geostationary satellites, which orbit high up above Earth, than for satellites in low-Earth orbit.

Types of satellites

Satellites are used for five main things: communication (relaying TV and phone signals), navigation (such as GPS—see pp. 118–119), meteorology (weather forecasting), Earth resources monitoring (for example measuring ocean temperatures), and military work. New satellites built by SpaceX are now being used as orbital WiFi routers to provide internet access.

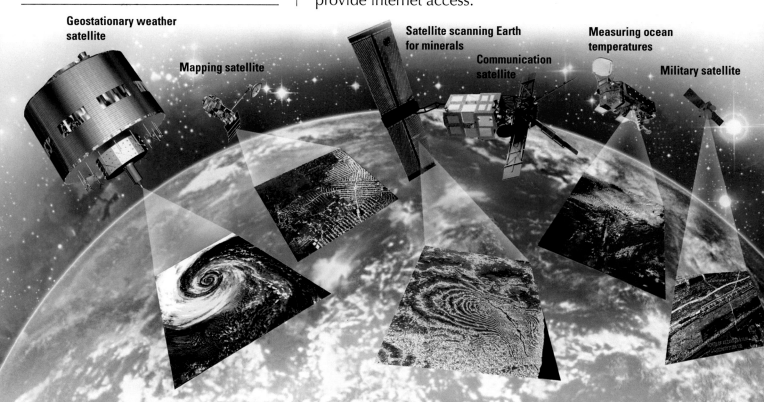

Geostationary weather satellite

Mapping satellite

Satellite scanning Earth for minerals

Communication satellite

Measuring ocean temperatures

Military satellite

GLOBAL POSITIONING

MANY YEARS AGO, PEOPLE USED MAPS, COMPASSES, AND THE STARS TO NAVIGATE—AND IT WAS STILL EASY TO GET LOST. NOW, GLOBAL POSITIONING SYSTEM (GPS) MAKES NAVIGATION SIMPLE.

GPS SATELLITES

Twenty-four GPS satellites constantly send out radio signals. By knowing the time that a signal was sent from a particular satellite and the time it is received, the receiver figures out the distance to that satellite. By using the distances from four satellites at once, the receiver can calculate its own position.

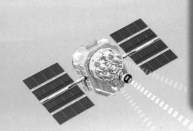

Cars often contain satellite-navigation systems that use GPS data as well as online maps to tell drivers where they are and how to get to their destinations. Some can also pass on reports about traffic conditions and suggest alternate routes.

There are six different GPS orbits, with four satellites sharing each one. At any moment, signals from at least four of them can be detected by a GPS receiver, wherever it is on Earth.

OTHER SYSTEMS

GPS is a U.S. system, but there are several others, including the Global Navigation Satellite System (GLONASS), which is Russian. Some equipment can receive signals from both GPS and GLONASS. Galileo is a global navigation satellite system currently being built by the European Union (EU) and European Space Agency (ESA).

GLONASS satellite

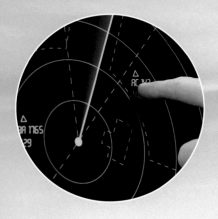

Increasingly, GPS data is used to help air-traffic controllers track aircraft.

A satellite-navigation system provides written and spoken directions as well as maps that show the driver where the car is.

GPS systems also work on hand-held communication devices such as cell phones and tablet computers.

Space stations

A space station is a satellite with people onboard, including: *Salyut 1* and *Mir* (both U.S.S.R.), *Skylab* (U.S.), *Tiangong* (Chinese), and the International Space Station (see pp. 122–123).

Space stations allow experiments to be carried out in microgravity conditions and astronomical observations to be made outside the atmosphere. The effects on humans in space can also be studied there.

Space-station concept

The first space station, *Salyut 1*, was launched into orbit in 1971. Because it was in a very low orbit, there was enough atmosphere present to slow it down, so it crashed back to Earth after five months. But it was very successful, and 22 cosmonauts (the Soviet term for astronaut) visited it, making up ten crews in all.

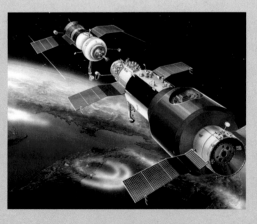

Left: *Skylab* was launched in 1973. Three crews, each with three astronauts, worked there.

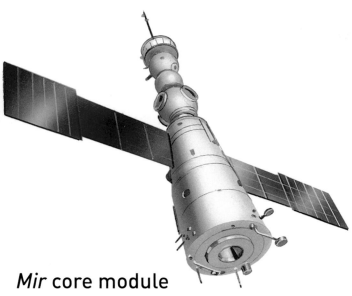

Mir core module

Mir was too large to be launched in one piece, so it was sent up in stages. The core module was launched in 1986, and it could house up to six cosmonauts. It remained in orbit for more than 15 years and made more than 76,000 Earth orbits.

Skylab before its heat shield and solar array (wing) was torn off

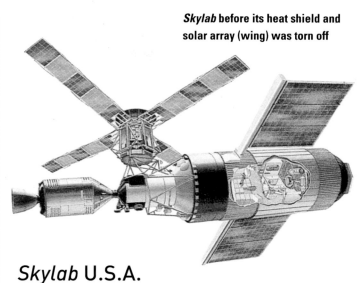

Skylab U.S.A.

Skylab was made partly from pieces of leftover *Apollo* spacecraft—its largest segment was made from the third stage of a *Saturn V* rocket. Its heat shield was torn off on its way to orbit, so astronauts had to build a new one to protect *Skylab* from the Sun's heat.

Putting *Mir* together

Over the next ten years, five modules were added to *Mir*, together with a special attachment to allow space shuttles to dock there. Special robotic *Progress* spacecraft ferried supplies to *Mir*, while crews arrived both by *Soyuz* craft and the space shuttle.

MEDIA

A BRICK-BUILT HOME IN SPACE

Space stations were written about in stories long before there were any in orbit. The first fictional station, made of brick, was described in an 1869 story by Edward Everett Hale (above). The space station was thrown into orbit by a huge spinning wheel.

SPACE LABORATORY

THE INTERNATIONAL SPACE STATION (ISS) IS A SCIENCE LABORATORY BUILT IN ORBIT BY 16 NATIONS. IT IS SO LARGE THAT IT CAN EASILY BE SEEN BY THE NAKED EYE FROM EARTH.

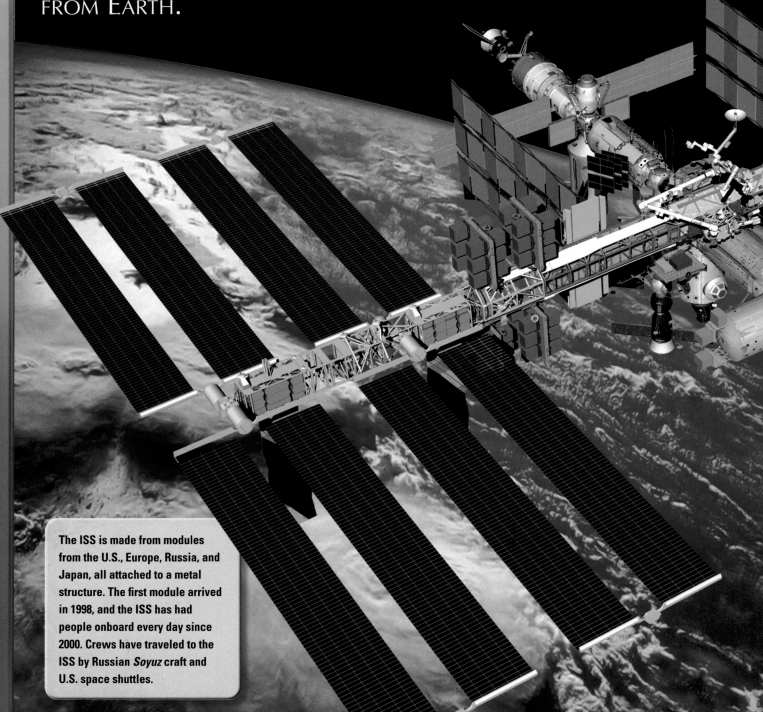

The ISS is made from modules from the U.S., Europe, Russia, and Japan, all attached to a metal structure. The first module arrived in 1998, and the ISS has had people onboard every day since 2000. Crews have traveled to the ISS by Russian *Soyuz* craft and U.S. space shuttles.

The ISS has huge solar panels that make electricity from sunlight. It takes 90 minutes to orbit Earth, and for 35 of those minutes, the Sun is hidden by Earth. While the Sun is hidden, the ISS runs on batteries. They are recharged when the Sun appears again.

SCIENCE IN SPACE

The ISS crews carry out experiments in many different areas, from space medicine and biology to weather forecasting and astronomy. On the ISS, the effects of microgravity on plant growth have been studied (see above).

WORKING IN SPACE

The crew members usually work ten hours each weekday and five hours on Saturdays. On the ISS, the Sun rises and sets 16 times every 24 hours. But the crew sticks to the same day and night periods as on Earth, sleeping for eight out of every 24 hours. There are soundproofed compartments for them, with sleeping bags attached to the walls.

Space probes

A space probe is a robotic machine sent to explore another planet or some other object in space. More than 100 have been launched. Probes have reached all of the planets, many moons, and several comets and asteroids.

Probes have many advantages over human explorers. They do not need much protection on their journeys, nor supplies of air or food. Also, they usually do not return to Earth, which saves a great deal of fuel.

Grand Tour
In the late 1900s, the giant planets Jupiter, Saturn, Uranus, and Neptune were all in roughly the same direction from Earth, so *Voyager 2* was able to visit them all. This mission was known as the Grand Tour.

TYPES OF PROBES

Flyby probes pass close to the objects they study, taking photographs and making measurements as they pass.

Orbiters travel around an object, collecting data over a long time.

Landers visit the surfaces of planets and moons but cannot move around on them.

Rovers crawl across the surfaces of planets to study them.

Sample return probes collect material from their destinations and send it back to Earth.

Below: The *Voyager 2* probe, which visited the four outer planets of the solar system

Flyby missions and orbiters
Flyby missions are the simplest and earliest types of probes. They are the only type to have explored Uranus and Neptune. Orbiters have visited Mercury, Venus, Mars, Jupiter, and Saturn, dwarf planets Ceres and Pluto, asteroids, the Moon, and the Sun.

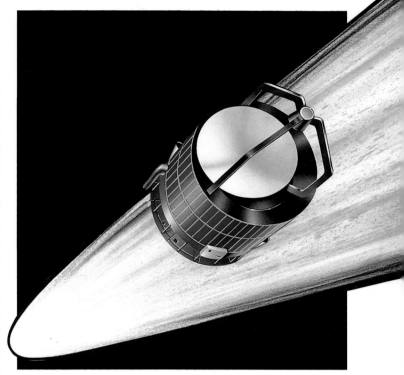

Venus multiprobe

The *Pioneer* Venus multiprobe sent four probes into the atmosphere of Venus in 1978. Each went to a different part of the planet. The probes were released from a "bus" that also fell through the atmosphere and made measurements of it on the way down.

Giotto

Giotto flew by Halley's Comet (see p. 63) in 1986. It was named after the painter Giotto, because he painted the comet in 1301. *Giotto* was expected to be destroyed by its visit so close to the comet. It was battered by high-speed dust particles that damaged it and sent it off course, but it survived to visit another comet called Grigg–Skjellerup in 1992.

Probe to Mercury

BepiColombo is a double probe that is scheduled to reach Mercury in 2025. One probe will map the planet and the other will study its magnetic field. *BepiColombo* will use a type of drive called solar electric propulsion, which is weaker than a rocket but works for years rather than minutes. It uses solar power to provide thrust.

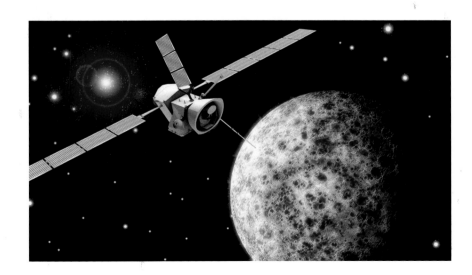

Landers and rovers

Landers have touched down on Venus, the Moon, Mars, Titan, a few asteroids and a comet. In 2015, the lander *Philae* from the ESA Rosetta mission successfully carried out the first soft landing on a comet.

Rovers are the most complicated probes of all and have been used only on the Moon and Mars. The Mars rovers had to make some decisions for themselves, because it took too long for radio instructions to travel to them from Earth.

ROVER FACTS
The dates refer to the touchdowns.

Moon
Lunokhod 1 (U.S.S.R.),
Sea of Rains,
November 17, 1970

Lunokhod 2 (U.S.S.R.),
Sea of Serenity,
January 15, 1973

Mars
Sojourner (U.S.),
Ares Vallis,
July 4, 1997

Spirit (U.S.),
Gusev crater,
January 3, 2004

Opportunity (U.S.),
Meridian Plain,
January 24, 2004

Curiosity (U.S.),
Gale crater,
August 5, 2012

Huygens on Titan
The *Cassini* orbiter released a car-size lander called *Huygens* that landed on Saturn's moon Titan in 2005. As it parachuted through the atmosphere (left), it sent back information about Titan and took pictures of the landscape. It took more than two hours to reach the surface.

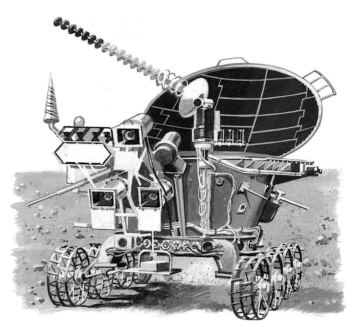

Sojourner

Parachutes, rockets, and air bags were all used to make sure *Sojourner* landed safely on Mars. The rover was equipped with a special device called an alpha proton x-ray spectrometer, which was used to find out exactly what the soil on Mars was made of.

Lunokhod 1 and *2*

Although the Americans put the first men on the Moon, the first robots to arrive there were Soviet. They were called *Lunokhod 1* and *2*, and they worked during the lunar day, powered by sunlight. The *Lunokhods* carried many instruments and measuring devices, including TV cameras. They also had special systems to ensure that they stopped automatically when in danger of falling over or overheating.

ExoMars

ExoMars is planned for launch in 2022. It is an advanced rover with the ability to drill down 6.5 ft. (2m) from the surface of Mars to take samples. It will analyze them in its own laboratory to search for traces of life. *ExoMars* will be able to determine its own routes across Mars by taking pictures of its surroundings and using them to make 3-D maps. The journey to Mars will take about nine months, and a parachute will be used to slow down *ExoMars'*s descent to the surface.

Exploration timeline

Long before the first spacecraft was built, scientists had figured out the math they needed to make it happen. In the few decades that have passed since then, spacecraft have traveled through the entire solar system.

1687 Sir Isaac Newton publishes his third law of motion: to every action there is an equal and opposite reaction. It is the most important law of space travel.
1883 Konstantin Tsiolkovsky publishes his theory on space rockets.
1926 Robert Goddard launches the world's first liquid-fueled rocket.
1957 *Sputnik 1*, the first artificial satellite, tests out space flight.
1957 The first living creature—a dog named Laika—is sent into orbit aboard *Sputnik 2*.
1959 *Luna 1* is launched, the first spacecraft to approach the Moon.
1959 *Luna 2* becomes the first artificial object to reach the Moon.
1960 *TIROS-1*, the first weather satellite, is launched into space.
1961 Russian Yuri Gagarin becomes the first human in space.
1961 J. F. Kennedy, the U.S. president, talks of a plan to reach the Moon by 1970.
1962 *Mariner 2* flies by Venus. It is the first probe to reach another planet.
1963 Russian Valentina Tereshkova becomes the first woman in space.
1964 The first three-person spacecraft, *Voskhod 1*, tests out living in space.
1965 Russian Alexei Leonov becomes the first person to walk in space.
1966 *Luna 9*, the first lander, arrives on the Moon.
1969 The *Apollo 11* mission takes humans onto the Moon for the first time.
1970 The first rover, *Lunokhod 1*, explores the Moon.
1971 The launch of the first space station—*Salyut 1*.
1971 *Mariner 9* becomes the first probe to orbit another planet (Mars).
1972 *Pioneer 10* is launched—the first probe to the outer planets.
1978 The first global positioning satellite is put into orbit.
1981 The first launch of the space shuttle—*Columbia*.
1984 The first space walks where astronauts are not tethered to their spacecraft.
1998 The launch of the first part of International Space Station (ISS).
2001 *NEAR Shoemaker* is the first probe to land on an asteroid.
2012 *Voyager 1* reaches interstellar space.
2014 *Philae* probe is the first to land on a comet.
2015 *Falcon 9* rocket is launched—the first reusable rocket.
2019 *Chang'e 4* performs first successful soft landing on the far side of the Moon.

A panorama of Santa Maria crater on Mars taken by exploration rover *Opportunity*

WEBSITES ABOUT SPACE TRAVEL

www.nasa.gov/audience/forkids/kidsclub/flash/index.html   Space games, news, and pictures.
www.spacekids.co.uk/spacehistory   History of space travel.
www.pbs.org/wgbh/nova/space/tour-solar-system.html   Virtual space travel.

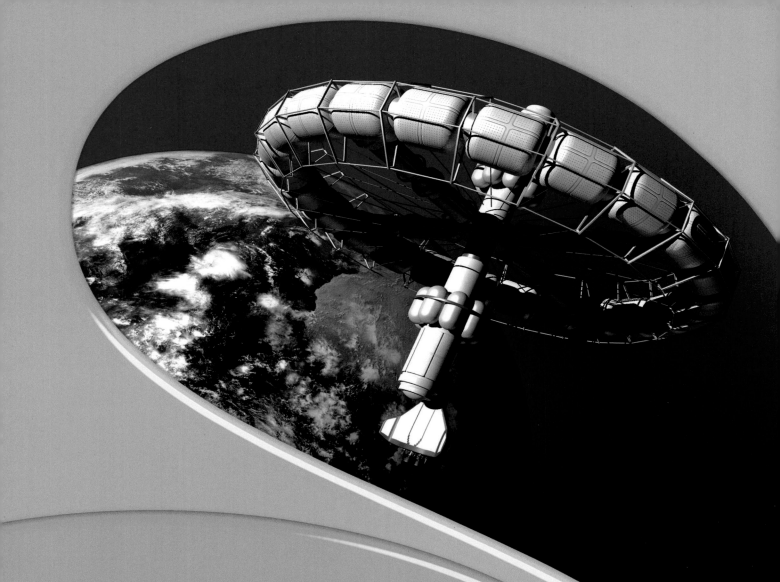

SPACE IN THE FUTURE

It has only been a few decades since the space age began, yet even in that short time, people have visited the Moon and sent probes throughout the entire solar system. However, the story of space exploration is only just beginning. No one can be sure where we will go in the future—or how we will get there—but here are a few ideas.

Space planes

A space plane is a vehicle that can fly through the air like a plane and also travel through space by rocket power. By far the most famous space plane was the space shuttle, but it was not the first, nor was it the last.

The space shuttle was an orbital space plane—this means that it was designed to reach a great enough height to go into orbit around Earth. Its last flight was in July 2011. Suborbital space planes do not need to fly as high.

First space plane

The first space plane was the *X-15*—a suborbital craft. A B-52 bomber carried it for the first part of its journey, and then its own rockets lifted it up into space.

VentureStar

VentureStar was intended to replace the space shuttle as a cheaper way of launching satellites than using rockets. It was a robotic craft that could carry people if required—but it was never built.

Right: The Boeing *X-37* is an experimental American robotic orbital space plane. It is lifted on an *Atlas V* rocket and lands like the space shuttle. It first flew in 2010 and has flown three missions since.

Above and left: *SpaceShipTwo* is a follow-up craft to *SpaceShipOne*, planned to carry passengers at a ticket price of around $200,000.

Future concepts for space planes

A new British space plane, *Skylon*, is being planned that would be the first spaceship ever to reach orbit without jettisoning fuel tanks along the way. *Skylon*'s engines could be used both within and beyond the atmosphere, and the space plane would be completely reusable.

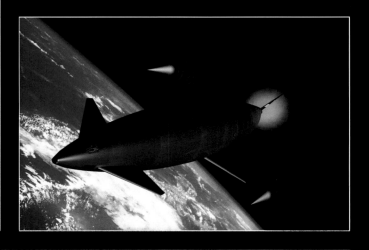

SpaceShips

Though early space planes were all government funded, some present and future ones are not. *SpaceShipOne* was the first successful privately funded suborbital space plane. It could carry two passengers as well as a pilot and was lifted up to a high altitude by a special carrier plane. It was completely paid for by Paul Allen, an American billionaire. A new version, *SpaceShipTwo*, (right) is due to be launched soon.

Mission to Mars

Mars is more than 140 times as far away from Earth as the Moon. So a mission to Mars will be longer, more complex, riskier, and more expensive than the *Apollo* Moon missions.

The latest plans for a trip to Mars are for the U.S. to launch a crewed spacecraft in the 2030s. The mission would take well over a year, including many weeks on Mars.

The mission
Robot craft would go to Mars first to test and prepare for the human landing that would follow months later. Fuel for the return journey would probably be made on Mars itself. The U.S., Russia, China, and the European Union (E.U.) have all planned spacecraft that could reach Mars.

Conditions on Mars
Mars is the most similar planet to Earth in our solar system—but it has a very thin atmosphere, and humans would need space suits in order to survive on its surface.

Above: Sunset on Mars, as photographed by a robot lander

Astronauts will use rover vehicles to move around and solar panels to generate electricity.

Mars craft

This is an artist's impression of a spacecraft that the U.S. space agency, the National Aeronautics and Space Administration (NASA), designed to travel to Mars. It is shown here blasting off from Earth's surface on its way to Mars.

Mars base

Astronauts on Mars, helped by robots, would need to build a base. At the base, plants and microbes would be grown inside greenhouses to provide both food and oxygen. Inside the base, the air pressure and temperature would be like those on Earth. Protection would be needed from dangerous radiation, which the atmosphere of Mars does not block.

MEDIA

MISSION TO MARS

In the 2000 science-fiction movie *Mission to Mars*, a team of astronauts and equipment is sent to the planet following a disaster during the first manned voyage there. Although conditions on Mars are harsher than those shown in the movie, the problems that the rescue team encountered were real, such as how to obtain food, water, and oxygen.

FUTURE SPACE DRIVES

So far, all spacecraft have relied on rocket power to leave Earth, and most have used it to complete their journeys. But rocket fuel is expensive and heavy, so other methods are being investigated.

SOLAR SAIL

The Sun constantly sends vast amounts of radiation into space. This radiation presses on everything it touches, and this pressure can be used to push large pieces of shiny material along. These are called solar sails.

The main problem with a solar sail is that it can be used only to move away from the Sun.

Below: Although the push of radiation pressure on the sail is quite small, the fact that it is constant—unlike rocket power—means that the sail keeps increasing in speed.

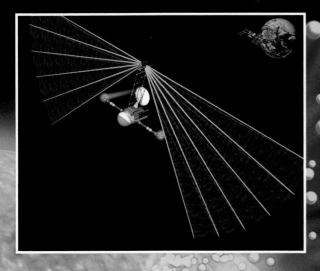

ION DRIVE

In an ion drive system, the outer particles, called electrons, are stripped from atoms to form ions. An electric field then squirts the ions out at high speeds, forcing the drive and spacecraft in the other direction. This type of drive has been tested on spacecraft.

Atoms are broken down into ions and electrons.

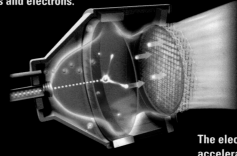

The electric field accelerates ions to generate thrust.

NUCLEAR DRIVE

Unlike ion drives and solar sails, nuclear drive systems can create strong thrust. The simplest type is based on nuclear fission, as used in nuclear power plants, but this creates pollution. Research is being carried out into a fusion device, which is cleaner and releases energy as the Sun does.

SPACE ELEVATOR

A geostationary satellite remains constantly 22,236 mi. (35,786km) above the same point on Earth. In theory, an enormous cable could stretch from it down to the ground, and people could travel up and down it in elevators.

Right: A nuclear-powered rocket of the future. It is streamlined to allow it to travel easily through Earth's atmosphere.

Mining the sky

So far, people have used space only as a place to study or for satellites to orbit. In the future, we may use it as a source of power and materials.

Using space in this way will be a great help for future space travelers, for people who remain on Earth, and, one day, for those who make their homes on other planets.

Solar power
Already, many spacecraft use solar cells to make electricity from sunlight. In the future, such solar power systems may be used on groups of satellites to collect power for use on Earth. It might be sent down from orbit in the form of laser beams or microwaves.

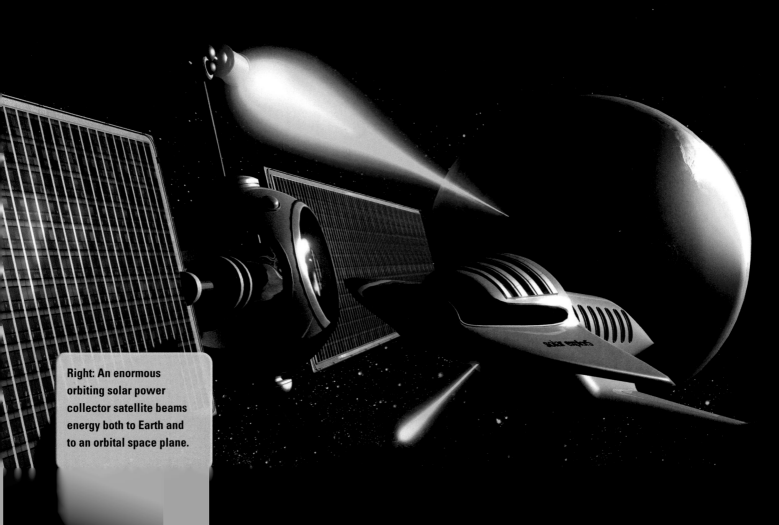

Right: An enormous orbiting solar power collector satellite beams energy both to Earth and to an orbital space plane.

Right: Robot space tugs pull an asteroid close to Earth to be mined, while an orbital solar array beams power to Earth.

Asteroid mining

Many asteroids contain useful metals and other substances, and their very low gravity means that little energy is needed to transport these materials to space destinations. The materials could also be used to build things in space or to produce drinkable water or rocket fuel for astronauts.

Water on the Moon

Space probes in 2009 and 2010 detected what are almost certainly thick ice layers on the Moon, close to the lunar north pole. There are probably at least 600 million tons of ice there, which will be essential for future Moon bases. The ice may either have formed on the Moon, arrived on comets, or both.

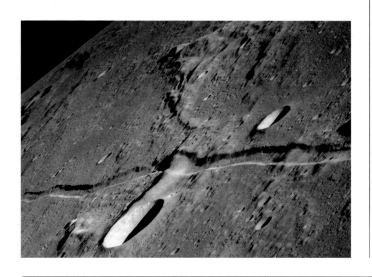

MEDIA

INTERSTELLAR

Interstellar, a 2014 movie, is set in the near future, where Earth is becoming uninhabitable. Scientists are trying to find Earthlike homes around other stars. They find a natural "wormhole" leading to a distant part of the universe and send spacecraft through. Although the movie goes far beyond known science, many parts are scientifically accurate.

MOON BASE

THERE ARE MANY REASONS WHY IT WOULD BE GOOD TO SET UP A BASE ON THE MOON. THE MOON IS A SOURCE OF VALUABLE MINERALS AND METALS, AND ITS LOW GRAVITY MAKES THEM EASY TO REMOVE. FOR THE SAME REASON IT WOULD ALSO BE A GOOD JUMPING-OFF POINT FOR MISSIONS TO OTHER PLANETS.

FORMS OF TRANSPORTATION

Astronauts would use electric vehicles to travel around the Moon's surface. Crewed and robot rockets and space planes could take useful metals back to Earth and crewed spacecraft could blast off from the Moon to Mars.

A NEW PERSPECTIVE ON SPACE

A moon base with a radio telescope might be built on the far side of the Moon. Because Earth is always below the horizon there, all radio interference from Earth would be blocked, so the observatory could study the much weaker radio signals from space.

LIVING QUARTERS

The moon base (below center) acts as a temporary home for the astronauts who work on the Moon. They stay at the base for a week or two before returning to Earth. The moon base has an air lock separating it from the lunar atmosphere to keep the air inside breathable and at a constant temperature.

A transporter (left) carries crew from a launching pad beyond the hills to the moon base (below).

An array of mirrors (below) directs sunlight onto a solar tower that generates electricity.

MARS STATION

REACHING MARS IS MUCH MORE DIFFICULT THAN
GOING TO THE MOON—BUT BECAUSE THE CONDITIONS
THERE ARE MORE SIMILAR TO THOSE ON EARTH,
A COLONY MIGHT BE EASIER TO BUILD.

**Right: A solar-powered radio
system keeps the colony in
touch with Earth.**

CHOOSING A SITE

Because Mars is colder than Earth, it might be best
to create a new colony near its equator. It might
be built at least partly underground, to protect
the astronauts from dangerous solar radiation
and extreme temperatures (both caused by the
lack of a thick atmosphere on Mars).

TERRAFORMING

In the distant future, it may be possible to terraform, or change the conditions on, Mars to make it more like Earth. Mirrors in orbit could reflect extra sunlight onto the surface to release frozen gases there. This would thicken the atmosphere and allow liquid water to exist on the surface. Then plants could grow and release oxygen into the air.

Below: Because the gravity on Mars is low and the wind is weak, structures would not have to be as sturdy as those on Earth.

MARS BASE LIFE

Mars is so far from Earth that as much as possible would have to be produced there, rather than be sent from Earth. The thin atmosphere would make it easy to use the energy of sunlight, though, and there is plenty of ice there to provide water.

Life in space

In a few billion years, the Sun will burn up the surface of Earth. If humans are to survive, they must leave before then to set up homes on a distant planet or in space.

The first step to abandoning Earth will be to transport building materials to bases. Once the bases are built, robots will be sent ahead to make the living conditions suitable for people.

Artificial gravity

The lack of gravity becomes very important on long space missions—bone and muscle weaken and blood changes, even with exercise. However, in a spinning spacecraft, the same effects as gravity are created. Things and people "stick" to the floor, like clothes do to the inside of a dryer.

Lonely journeys

Anyone who lives in space will need to take everything they have with them—the only thing available to space travelers is the power of sunlight, and that becomes weaker as the Sun is left behind.

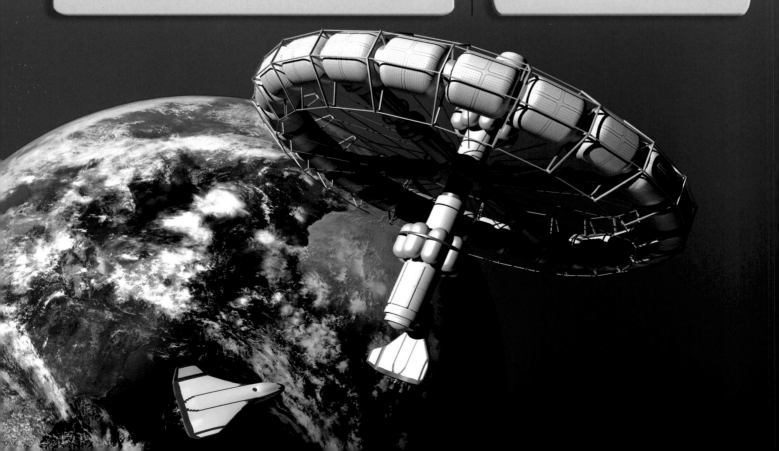

Space recycling

Rather than taking enormous amounts of food and air with them, large space stations could take plants instead. As well as providing food, plants release oxygen for people to breathe. They take in waste gases, too. Plants could even be used to make parks and gardens for the astronauts to enjoy.

Star spheres

In the distant future, many people could live on the insides of spheres built around stars. Or such spheres could be used to capture all of the energy of a star's radiation and supply the enormous energy that spacecraft need to reach high speed quickly. The spheres would have to be made of many separate orbiting sections.

Generation starships

One way of reaching the stars is by a generation starship. The original large crew would live their whole lives onboard, and so would their children and grandchildren; only their distant descendants might actually reach the stars. Such craft would have to be enormous, as they would be the entire world for the travelers. A starship would be completely cut off from Earth, so the crew would have to solve their own problems and make their own decisions about where to end their voyage.

Starships

It is not difficult to make an interstellar spacecraft (starship): the *Pioneer, Voyager,* and *New Horizons* probes will eventually reach other stars. The main challenge for star travel is the time it will take to make the journey—more than a human lifetime.

Anyone traveling to another star would be very cut off from Earth. With even the closest star, it would take more than eight years to receive a reply to a radio message. One solution for star travel is for generations of people to be born in space to survive the journey.

Planet-exploration craft
A starship would be too big to land on another world, so it would carry shuttle craft with it to journey down to the planets it reaches (below) while it either remains in orbit or continues on its way.

Cold journeys
Small animals can be deep frozen and then revived. This may be possible for people, too, and would be another way of coping with long space journeys. Each of the small pods in this cutaway would contain a single crew member.

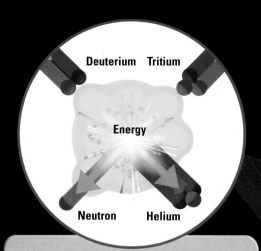

Deuterium   Tritium

Energy

Neutron   Helium

Fusion power

Starlight is produced when merging atoms release energy. Similar nuclear fusion processes may be used to power starships. Merging deuterium and tritium atoms—two forms of hydrogen— produce helium and atomic particles called neutrons and release a lot of usable energy.

Left: The red section is a metal framework that uses a huge electric field to capture electrically charged space particles. This creates reaction mass (see below left).

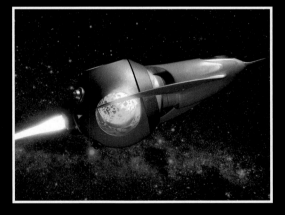

Interstellar ramjet

As well as fuel, spacecraft need "reaction mass." This is material that is squirted out behind them to move them forward. An interstellar ramjet (right) collects the very thin gas in space to use as reaction mass.

Antimatter starships

Antimatter is a material that is the opposite of ordinary matter. When it comes in contact with ordinary matter, a vast amount of energy appears—more than from any other fuel and enough to power a huge starship. Scientists can make antimatter, but only in laboratories.

LIFE ELSEWHERE

MANY STARS HAVE PLANETS MOVING AROUND THEM—THE FIRST SUCH EXOPLANET WAS FOUND IN 1992 AND THE CURRENT TOTAL OF KNOWN PLANETS IS 4,144. ALTHOUGH NO GENUINELY EARTH-LIKE EXOPLANETS HAVE BEEN DISCOVERED, SOME ARE VERY SIMILAR TO EARTH IN SIZE AND DISTANCE FROM THEIR SUN-LIKE STAR.

WHAT ARE ALIENS LIKE?

As yet, no life forms have been found on other planets. If they exist, it is almost certain that they have evolved to fit into the conditions in which they live, but we have no idea what they would look like. They might look as different as an eagle does from an oak tree. Some might be much smarter than we are or be bigger and stronger.

A WORLD IN THE CLOUDS

On Earth, living things exist in boiling water, icy seas, and high up in the sky. Alien life forms might survive in equally harsh environments. The above picture shows the possible inhabitants of a thick, warm atmosphere surrounding a distant planet.

WATER WORLD

Deep under Earth's oceans there are living things that rely on volcanic activity for the energy they need. There are moons in our solar system with oceans underneath their frozen surfaces, too, and there may be many other worlds like this in space— with their own populations of living things.

In this imaginary image, a spacecraft has landed on an ice-covered world and has sent a robot explorer to melt its way through to explore the ocean beneath.

X720 PROBE

X721 SUBMERSIBLE

The creatures here might communicate and hunt by using patterns of lights that are made by chemicals in their bodies.

In touch with aliens

For a long time, people have looked up at the night sky and wondered, "Are we alone in the universe?" Though most people think we are not, no good evidence of alien life has yet been found.

Scientists have been listening for radio signals from other civilizations for many years, and some have sent signals out into space, too.

Visitors from space

Perhaps one day an alien spacecraft will visit Earth, as has happened in many science-fiction movies. An alien spacecraft may not look the same as ours and could be powered differently.

UFOs

Unexplained lights in the sky are called unidentified flying objects (UFOs), but there is no evidence that they are actually alien spacecraft. In 1995, an untitled hoax movie was released that was supposed to show alien corpses being studied.

Left: This imaginary spacecraft is sending a small shuttle craft down from orbit to explore Earth.

Listening for life

Many radio telescopes have been used to listen for signals from aliens, including this one in Arecibo, Puerto Rico. Projects like these are called SETI (search for extraterrestrial intelligence). The most interesting result so far happened in 1977, when a sudden burst of radio waves was picked up by Ohio State University's Big Ear telescope. It is called the Wow! signal because that is what the observer wrote on the telescope printout. No one has been able to explain the Wow! signal properly.

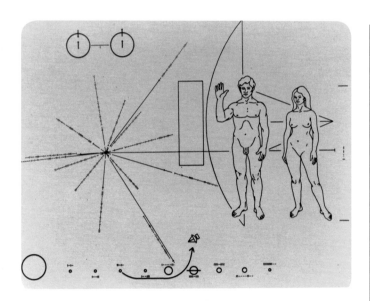

Pioneer plaques

In tens of thousands of years, the *Pioneer* and *Voyager* probes will pass close to other star systems. The *Pioneer* craft carry plaques (above) with messages to any aliens that might encounter them, showing where Earth is. Pictures of people are shown, too. The *Voyager* probes carry gold disks containing pictures and sounds from Earth.

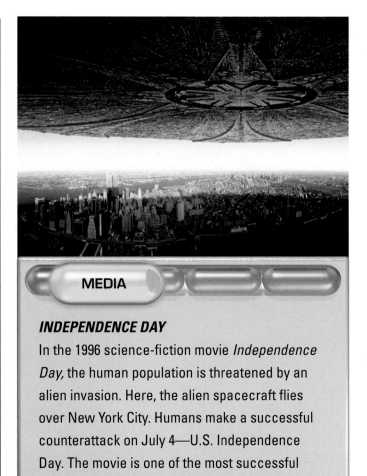

MEDIA

INDEPENDENCE DAY

In the 1996 science-fiction movie *Independence Day,* the human population is threatened by an alien invasion. Here, the alien spacecraft flies over New York City. Humans make a successful counterattack on July 4—U.S. Independence Day. The movie is one of the most successful disaster films ever produced.

Beyond time and space

In 1905, Albert Einstein published a paper showing that time flows at different rates for people moving at different speeds, rather than being the same for everyone everywhere.

The discovery that time is not a constant revolutionized physics. Within a few years, Einstein had shown that gravity can also change the way time flows. Using his theories, astronomers have been able to explain many of the strange objects they can see in space.

EINSTEIN

Albert Einstein, born in 1875, changed many areas of science. He developed an area of physics called relativity that offered a new explanation of space, time, matter, and energy. Einstein used relativity to develop the first mathematical theory of the entire universe and to figure out the most famous equation in the world—$E = mc^2$—where E = energy, m = mass, and c = the speed of light. It shows that matter can appear as vast amounts of energy. It led to the development of nuclear power and nuclear weapons.

Space-time

One of Einstein's key discoveries was that space and time are actually different ways of looking at the same thing—called space-time. The way gravity works can be explained in terms of space-time.

Warps in space-time

Massive objects warp (bend) the space-time around them, and the more concentrated their mass is, the greater the warping effect. This is why the shapes of distant galaxies can look strange: their light is distorted because it passes through the warped space-time surrounding massive objects on its way to Earth.

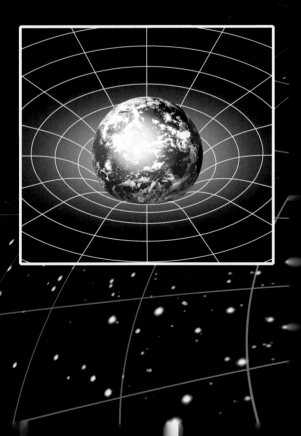

Wormholes

Einstein's theories predict the possibility of "tunnels" through space-time called wormholes. If they exist, they must be tiny, but it may be possible in the future to locate and expand them, making shortcuts to distant places or even other times.

Natural time machines

The usual fate of travelers who approach a black hole too closely is to be crushed, but if the black hole is spinning and they choose the correct path, they may travel close to it without being destroyed. Some scientists believe that this would allow black holes to be used to travel through space. Whether or not the space travelers could return home to Earth is as yet unknown.

Unanswered questions

We can reach only a tiny fraction of the universe by spacecraft. For information about the rest, we must analyze the light and other radiation from objects in space.

It is not surprising that many questions about the universe remain, but science has already solved many of its mysteries. One day, it will probably solve them all. Here are some current mysteries.

Dark matter

We can determine the masses of galaxies in two ways: by measuring the effects of their gravity or by counting the stars in them. But the answers are very different—which means that most of the mass of every galaxy is in the form of a mysterious "dark matter" that may take the form of small stars or subatomic particles.

UNIVERSAL MYSTERIES

The biggest question about the universe is, Where did it come from? Although we understand more or less the whole history of the universe from the big bang until the present, no one knows why the big bang itself happened.

We also do not know for sure if our universe really is all there is. It is possible that it is only one of many universes but that we cannot see or reach any of the others.

Below: The mass of these galaxies and hot gas (pink) is greater than can be explained by the number of stars present. The rest is due to dark matter.

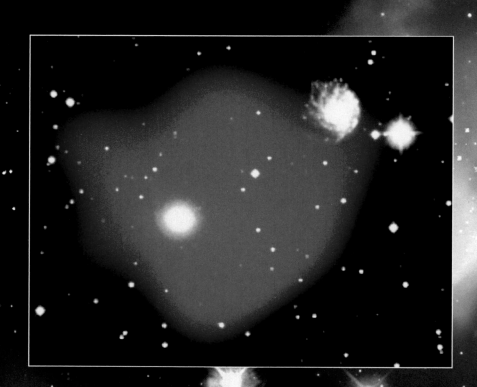

Dark energy

In the late 1990s, observation and analysis of the universe showed that it is expanding faster and faster—so something must be pushing it apart. This something is dark energy, a mysterious force that makes up about three-fourths of the universe. It seems to be a little like gravity, but instead of pulling, it pushes.

Missing metal

Everything in the universe is made from around 100 different elements. These include metals, such as iron and gold. Astronomers have worked out how the elements were made and how much of each element there should be. The exception is lithium—there is much less of this metal than anyone can explain.

Further facts

Although science-fiction books and movies are mostly for fun, some are based on real science, like most of the ones listed here. If you want only the facts, any of the TV series listed in the third column are a good place to start.

BOOKS
- *From the Earth to the Moon* and *Round the Moon* by Jules Verne (1865 and 1870): the first reasonably scientific books about what a Moon voyage might be like.
- *The First Men in the Moon* by H. G. Wells (1901): a Moon adventure that might have been.
- *The Black Cloud* by Sir Fred Hoyle (1957): a very strange cosmic event, imagined by a top British scientist.
- *Welcome to Mars!* by James Blish (1967): an exciting story about a young inventor's trip to Mars.
- *Cosmic* by Frank Cottrell Boyce (2008): a fun book about an accidental space adventure.

MOVIES
- *Destination Moon* (1950): an accurate prediction of the Moon landings that took place years later.
- *The Day the Earth Stood Still* (1951): one of the best "alien visits Earth" film depictions.
- *2001: A Space Odyssey* (1968): this movie is still realistic and thought provoking today.
- *Apollo 13* (1995): a fictionalized account of a real drama in space.
- *Contact* (1997): what might happen if a project to pick up alien broadcasts was successful.
- *Gravity* (2013): largely accurate movie about being stranded in space.

FACTUAL TV SERIES
- *Cosmos* (1980): written and presented by top space scientist Carl Sagan.
- *From the Earth to the Moon* (1998): a miniseries about the Moon landings.
- *Voyage to the Planets and Beyond* (2004): though fiction, this two-part BBC series about a future journey of exploration of the solar system was made as realistic as possible.
- *In the Shadow of the Moon* (2006): the story of the *Apollo* missions, by the astronauts and controllers involved.
- *Wonders of the Solar System* (2010): explores the far reaches of the universe.

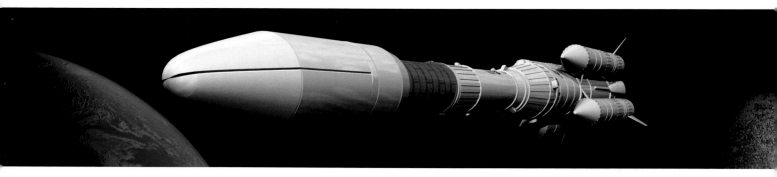

An impression of a futuristic rocket with payload in space

WEBSITES ABOUT SPACE AND TIME

https://www.theguardian.com/books/childrens-sci-fi Children's books, especially science fiction.

http://sfbook.com Science-fiction book reviews.

www.filmsite.org/sci-fifilms.html All about science-fiction movies.

www.imdb.com/chart/moviemeter Filter by Sci-Fi for th most popular science-fiction movies.

Glossary

altitude The height of an object above the surface of Earth or other world.

asteroid A rocky body that circles the Sun. Most asteroids are found between the orbits of Mars and Jupiter. Asteroids are so small that their gravity is too weak to pull them into spherical (round) shapes.

astronomer A person who studies objects in space.

atmosphere The layer of gases and clouds that surround a star, planet, or moon. Earth's atmosphere is called air.

atoms Tiny objects, much too small to see, of which everything is made. Atoms combine to make molecules.

aurora The glow in the sky seen near the north or south pole of Earth or other planet.

axis An imaginary line going through the center of an object, around which it spins.

big bang The sudden expansion with which the universe began, according to modern theory.

billion One thousand million (1,000,000,000).

black hole The remains of a star that pulls in any object around it in space, even rays of light, so that it appears black.

cabin The part of a vehicle in which people travel.

celestial sphere The imaginary hollow sphere surrounding Earth that seems to turn from east to west, carrying the stars along with it.

cluster A group of stars or galaxies held together by gravity.

comet A mass of ice and dust. Sometimes, when a comet travels toward the Sun, the Sun's heat turns some of the ice into gas and releases some of the dust, forming two tails.

constellation A group of stars in the sky. Usually, the stars are not actually grouped together but are at different distances from Earth. They seem close only because they are in more or less the same direction from us.

core The central part of a planet, star, or other object.

corona A very hot and deep but very low-density layer of gas around the Sun or other star.

crater A deep, bowl-shaped area on the surface of a planet or other world. Craters are sometimes caused by volcanoes but more often by the impacts of meteorites, comets, or other objects.

density The amount of mass in a particular volume.

dwarf planet A world that is smaller than a planet but that has enough gravity to give it a roughly spherical (round) shape.

Earth The planet we live on and the third from the Sun. The only planet with a single moon and liquid oceans.

electron An electrically charged particle that forms part of an atom.

equator The imaginary line drawn around the middle of a star, planet, or other world.

equatorial radius The distance from the center of a planet or other spherical world to its equator.

evolve To develop from one type of thing to another; usually refers to living things.

extrasolar planet A planet that orbits a star other than the Sun.

force A push or a pull.

galaxy A collection of millions, billions, or trillions of stars held together by gravity.

gamma rays The most powerful type of radiation.

gravity The force with which every object pulls on every other object.

horizon The line where the sky meets the land or ocean.

infrared A type of radiation that can often be felt as heat.

interstellar Between stars.

ion An atom with one or more electrons taken from or added to it, leaving it charged with electricity.

jettison To throw away from a vehicle.

lander An uncrewed or robot spacecraft that lands on another world to explore it but that cannot move around on its surface.

laser A device that makes a beam of light that is very narrow, does not spread out much as it moves, and is of exactly one color.

light-minute The distance traveled by light in one minute.

light-year The distance traveled by light in one year.

lunar Having to do with the Moon.

magnetic field The area around a magnet (or a planet, star, or other world) where magnetism can be detected.

Mars The fourth planet from the Sun, the second smallest, and the one most similar to Earth.

mental Having to do with the mind.

Mercury The closest planet to the Sun and also the smallest.

meteor A streak of light in the sky caused by a meteoroid burning up as it falls through Earth's atmosphere.

meteorite A piece of stone or metal that reaches Earth after falling from space.

meteoroid An object drifting in space that may fall through the atmosphere to make a meteor.

microgravity The tiny gravity force that is felt inside spacecraft.

microwaves A powerful type of radio wave.

Milky Way The name of the galaxy of which our Sun is a member.

moon A world that orbits a planet or asteroid. Also known as a natural satellite.

navigate To find your way or course when traveling.

nebula A cloud of dust and gas out in space.

nuclear Having to do with the nuclei (cores) of atoms.

nuclear fission A process by which the nuclei of very large atoms break apart and release energy. Used in nuclear power plants and some nuclear weapons.

nuclear fusion A process by which the nuclei of hydrogen atoms merge and release energy. Powers many stars and some nuclear weapons.

orbit The path of one object around another object in space.

particle A tiny object, such as a grain of dust, an atom, or an electron.

planet A large world, often with an atmosphere, that moves around the Sun or another star. Some planets have moons.

plaque A smooth piece of metal or other hard material, usually with words or pictures on it.

pole One of two "ends" of a planet, around which it spins. Magnetic poles are the two parts of a magnet or star or planet where the magnetic field is strongest.

probe A spacecraft with no crew onboard, sent to explore objects in space.

radar A system in which microwaves are bounced off objects to find out about them.

radiation A type of energy that travels at a very high speed.

radio waves A type of radiation used to transmit messages and also made naturally by many objects in space.

robot A complicated machine that carries out a range of tasks,
often ones that a human would otherwise do.

rotation period The time a planet, star, or other object in space takes to turn around once. The rotation period of Earth is one day.

rover A type of electric car used to explore the Moon, or a robot that can move around the surface of another world to explore it.

satellite An object, either natural or artificial (made by people), that orbits a planet or other object in space.

solar Having to do with the Sun.

solar system The Sun and all of the planets and other objects
that move around it.

space The area beyond Earth's atmosphere.

supernova An extremely bright explosion, sometimes the result of the death of a star.

temperature A measure in degrees of how hot or cold something is.

trillion One million million (1,000,000,000,000).

ultraviolet A powerful type of radiation that can cause a suntan or sunburn.

universe Everything that exists.

x-ray A very powerful type of radiation that can pass through small objects.

Index

Acknowledgments

The Publisher would like to thank the following illustrators: Sebastian Quigley (Linden Artists) Sam and Steve Weston (Linden Artists).

The Publisher would like to thank the following for permission to reproduce their material. Every care has been taken to trace copyright holders.

top = t; bottom = b; center = c; left = l; right = r

Pages 4 Shutterstock/Giovanni Benintende; 10 Shutterstock/AJP; 11 Shutterstock/Pi-Lens; 13 Corbis/Kennan Ward; 15l Shutterstock/Ozerov Alexander; 15r Art Archive/Superstock; 19 Shutterstock/Antonio Abrignani; 21 Shutterstock/RG Meier; 24-25 Shutterstock/carlos martin diaz; 25r SPL/David Parker; 26 iStock/ bjdlzx; 27tl Shutterstock/fstockfoto; 27bl Alamy/World History Archive; 27br Kobal Collection/Columbia; 29c Getty/Claudio Giovanni/Stringer; 29b Kamioka Observatory/ICRR (Instutute for Cosmic Ray Research), The University of Tokyo; 33 iStock/ewg3D; 39tr NASA/Johns Hopkins University Applied Physics Laboratory/ Carnegie Institution of Washington; 45t Shutterstock/Vibrant Image Studio; 45b Shutterstock/Danshutter; 48, 51 NASA; 55tl SPL/Mark Garlick; 55cr /NASA; 56 Shutterstock/Diego Barucco; 57 Alamy/epa European pressphoto agency b.v.; 59 NASA; 60bl Shutterstock/Dmitriy Kovtun; 60br Shutterstock/Jeffrey M. Frank; 60cr Getty/Image North America; 61 Getty/Tony Hallas; 62 iStock/ MARHARYTA MARKO; 63l NASA/ ESA; 63r SPL/David A. Hardy; 64 Shutterstock/dedek; 67 SPL/Christian Darkin; 68 Shutterstock/Serg64; 73 Shutterstock/xfox01; 77 NASA; 77r SPL/ SAKKMESTERKE; 78 ESO/EHT Collaboration; 83 SPL/Mark Garlick; 85 NASA; 86 Shutterstock/William Attard Mccarthy; 87tr SPL/ EUROPEAN SOUTHERN OBSERVATORY; 87t iStock/Manfred_Konrad; 88 Hubble; 88r SPL/DR FRED ESPENAK; 89 Kobal Collection/Paramount; 92bc iStock/3quarks; 93l Shutterstock/Richard Williamson; 93c NASA; 95b SPL/CARLOS CLARIVAN; 98l Shutterstock/Zastol'skiy Victor Leonidovich; 98r Bridgeman/Bibliotheque des Arts Decoratifs, France/ Archives Charmet; 99l Alamy/AF Archive; 99t NASA; 99r Rex/ITV; 100-101 SPL/SPACEX; 101tr SPL/MARK WILLIAMSON; 104 Alamy/SPUTNIK; 117 Shutterstock/Vadim Ponomarenko; 119t Shutterstock/Jirsak; 119l Shutterstock/kaczor58; 119r Shutterstock/Evgeny Vasenev; 120 NASA; 121 Alamy/Granger Historical Picture Archive; 122 Shutterstock/jean-luc; 123 NASA; 133t, b NASA; 133r Kobal Collection/Touchstone; 137 Alamy/ AF Archive; 148 Shutterstock/photoBeard; 149t Shutterstock/Israel Pabon; 149c Kobal Collection/Twentieth Century-Fox; 152 Shutterstock/Neo Edmund; 152r NASA; 154 Shutterstock/1971yes.